Reading Through History
The Cold War
From the Rise of Communism to the Collapse of the Soviet Union

By Jake Henderson and Robert Marshall

The Cold War
By Jake Henderson& Robert Marshall

ISBN-13: 9781722934897
ISBN-10: 1722934891

Reading Through History

The Cold War:

Communism

For many years, communism was the dominant economic system used in many countries across Eastern Europe and Asia. But, what is communism? How did it get started?

The modern idea of communism was first proposed by German philosophers Karl Marx and Friedrich Engels. Together, they wrote a short book known as "The Communist Manifesto". In it, they suggested that someday, the working class, known as the proletariat, would rise up and overthrow their wealthy employers. At that point, the proletariat would completely restructure society.

Karl Marx

One of the key principles of communism is the concept of a classless society. This led to a concerted effort by communist governments to eliminate anything that might be representative of class warfare, or create class envy. For example, clothing in communist nations was relatively bland and uniformed, and most cars were of the same make.

More importantly, the salaries of employees, regardless of the job performed, were all regulated so that each person would earn approximately the same amount of money. The eventual goal of this 'classless society' would be a state in which there was no currency at all, and the government provided food, clothing and shelter to citizens in equal amounts.

In a true communist nation, there is to be no private ownership of property. All property and businesses are owned by the national government. Therefore, all workers are employed by the government. This would also mean that the state controlled all means of producing goods and services, thus allowing the government to control the distribution of those products.

Marx and Engels' arguments in favor of a classless society gained popularity throughout the later part of the 19th Century. Finally, in 1917, a group of Communists in Russia, known as Bolsheviks, started a revolution. The end result was a Communist takeover of Russia and the creation of a nation known as the Soviet Union.

For many years, the Soviet Union was the only Communist nation. However, following World War II, many other Eastern European nations followed Russia's lead and implemented a communist system. These nations included Poland, Czechoslovakia, East Germany, Hungary, Bulgaria, and Romania.

Throughout the 1940s, '50s and '60s, many Asian nations such as China and North Korea also adopted Communism. At one point during what came to be known as the Cold War era, a full ¼ of the world's population lived under some type of communist rule.

The Soviet Union

During the Cold War, the United States and the Soviet Union were the world's only two "super powers". But where was the Soviet Union? Why doesn't it still exist today?

The Hammer and Sickle

The Soviet Union was, at one time, the largest nation on the planet. It consisted of the modern nations of Russia, Ukraine, Moldova, Belarus, Armenia, Azerbaijan, Georgia, Kazakhstan, Tajikistan, Uzbekistan, Turkmenistan, Kyrgyzstan, Latvia, Lithuania, and Estonia. It spanned more than 6,200 miles from east to west and included 11 time zones.

The Soviet Union was officially known as the Union of the Soviet Socialist Republics, and it was created in 1922. Five years prior, in 1917, a revolution was orchestrated in Russia by a man named Vladimir Lenin and his followers known as the Bolsheviks.

Following this revolution, a civil war erupted between the Bolsheviks and other factions fighting for control of Russia. In 1922, the Bolshevik Army, known as the Red Army, gained control and formally changed the name of the country to the Soviet Union (or USSR).

In 1924, Joseph Stalin became the leader and maintained that position until his death in 1953. Stalin led the Soviet Union through a period of rapid industrialization in an attempt to modernize the nation. However, Stalin was also a brutal dictator who killed millions of his own citizens in order to maintain power and implement his policies.

In 1941, Nazi Germany invaded the Soviet Union, bringing the USSR into World War II as an ally of Great Britain (and later the United States). After four long years of fighting, the Allied Powers defeated Germany and their Axis allies. The USA and the USSR emerged as the world's two super powers.

Joseph Stalin

In the late 1940s and early '50s, the two nations quickly became adversaries, especially after the Soviet Union successfully tested its first atomic bomb in 1949. This weapon gave each nation the ability to inflict massive amounts of damage upon and potentially destroy the other. This marked the beginning of the forty year struggle known as the Cold War.

After an almost fifty year standoff with the United States, the Cold War ended in 1991 when the Soviet Union finally collapsed. The remnants of that once powerful nation include the present day nation of Russia, as well as 14 other smaller nations.

Multiple Choice: *Please answer the following questions related to the passages you just read:*

1._____ The title of the book written by Karl Marx and Friedrich Engels was?
a. Crime and Punishment
b. The Wealth of Nations
c. The Communist Manifesto
d. Birth of a Nation

2._____ One of the key principles of communism is?
a. A classless society
b. Private ownership of businesses
c. Individual property rights
d. Emphasis on individuality

3._____ The eventual goal of a classless society would be?
a. A society with no currency at all
b. A society in which the government provided food and clothing for all citizens
c. A society in which the government provided shelter for all citizens
d. The eventual goal of a classless society would be to provide all of these things

4._____ Which of the following is true in a communist nation?
a. Personal freedom and liberty are highly valued
b. All property and businesses are owned by the national government
c. Distribution of products is not regulated by the government
d. Employees have a wide range of salaries depending on the job they perform

5._____ The first nation in which a communist revolution took place was?
a. Russia
b. Germany
c. France
d. The United States of America

6._____ The modern day nations of Russia, Ukraine, Belarus and twelve others created what nation?
a. The Warsaw Pact
b. The Soviet Union
c. The Holy Roman Empire
d. The Eurasian Alliance

7._____ The initials USSR stand for?
a. Union of the Socialist States of Russia
b. United States of Socialist Russia
c. Union of the Soviet Socialist Republics
d. Unified States of Socialist Regions

8._____ In 1924, who became the leader of the Soviet Union?
a. Vladimir Lenin
b. Leon Trotsky
c. Nikita Khrushchev
d. Joseph Stalin

9._____ During World War II, the Soviet Union was allied with which two nations?
a. Great Britain & the United States
b. Germany & Italy
c. Japan & China
d. France & Italy

10._____ Which of the following events occurred in 1991?
a. 1991 was the year the Soviet Union was created
b. 1991 was the year the US and the Soviet Union officially opened trade relations
c. 1991 was the year the Soviet Union collapsed
d. 1991 was the year when war began between the US and the Soviet Union

Free Response Questions for Communism and the Soviet Union:

1) Describe your opinion on the concept of communism. Do you feel that a TRUE communist state could ever be achieved? Why or why not?

2) Why do you believe that the ideas of communism might have been appealing to many of the lower class (poorer) citizens? How do you think most of the wealthier (richer) people would have felt about it?

3) Why do you think the Soviet Union and the United States became adversaries/enemies after the end of WWII? Is it possible for two powerful nations with opposing types of governments to stay allies? Explain why or why not?

Cold War Vocabulary: Communism and the Soviet Union

a. Cold War
b. The Proletariat
c. Communism
d. The Soviet Union
e. Vladimir Lenin

f. Bolsheviks
g. Karl Marx
h. Industrialization
i. The Communist Manifesto
j. Adversaries

1._____   Leader of the Bolsheviks who established communism in Russia.

2._____   An economic theory proposed by Karl Marx which stresses a classless society and government ownership of property.

3._____   He wrote the Communist Manifesto and first proposed the concept of communism.

4._____   The working class.

5._____   People or groups who oppose one another in a contest or war.

6._____   The conversion to advanced methods of manufacturing.

7._____   A short book written by Karl Marx and Friedrich Engels, in which they proposed the theory of communism.

8._____   A group of Communists in Russia who started a revolution and took control of the government.

9._____   The name given to Russia from 1922 to 1991, during the Communist rule of Russia.

10._____   A war of suspicion, hostility and threats, but no actual fighting.

Cold War Vocabulary: Fill in the Blank
Use the words from the word bank, and write in the correct choice to complete the sentence.

a. Cold War
b. The Proletariat
c. Communism
d. The Soviet Union
e. Vladimir Lenin

f. Bolsheviks
g. Karl Marx
h. Industrialization
i. The Communist Manifesto
j. Adversaries

1. Karl Marx suggested that someday the _____ would rise up and overthrow their rich oppressors.

2. The United States and the Soviet Union fought a _____ from the 1950s through the 1980s.

3._____ and Friedrich Engels wrote the Communist Manifesto.

4. The Bolsheviks were led by _____.

5. Throughout the Cold War, the United States and the Soviet Union were _____.

6. Karl Marx was the first to propose the theory of _____.

7. The _____ led a revolution in Russia and took control of the country.

8. The Soviet Union was able to undergo a period of _____ under the leadership of Joseph Stalin.

9. The book written by Karl Marx and Friedrich Engels is known as _____.

10. The name given to Russia after the communists seized control of Russia was _____.

The Berlin Airlift

One of the first major incidents during the Cold War became known as the Berlin Airlift. So, what was the Berlin Airlift, and why was it started?

At the conclusion of World War II, Germany was divided into four portions. The United States, Great Britain, France, and the Soviet Union each controlled one segment. The city of Berlin, which was located in the Soviet sector, was also split into four similar segments. The American, British, and French portions joined together to create West Berlin, while the Soviet region was known as East Berlin.

In 1948, the American, British, and French regions of Germany announced that they would be creating, and using, a new currency called the Deutsche Mark. This would replace the old German currency known as the Reich Mark.

In response to this decision, the Soviet Union halted all traffic between East Berlin and West Berlin. They also severed all communications with the non-Soviet sectors of Berlin. Supply trains were turned around and even the electricity was cut from West Berlin.

Since Berlin was located 100 miles inside the Soviet sector of Germany, this meant that the non-Soviet region of Berlin was completely isolated in a hostile territory. At the time, this region of Berlin had enough food to last about 36 days and nearly 45 days' worth of coal.

By June 24th, 1948, West Berlin was completely cut off from the rest of the world and surrounded by 2.5 million Soviet troops. On June 25th, the US, Great Britain and other allied nations decided on a response. It would become known as the Berlin Airlift.

The Allies began flying planes into West Berlin, each one carrying loads of supplies, including food, coal and other necessities. At first, progress was slow, but before long, fresh supplies were flowing into West Berlin by the minute.

The Soviets were helpless to stop the flights. If they had opened fire on the planes, it would have been considered an act of war. So, the planes were allowed to land, supplying West Berliners with the items and food they needed.

By April of 1949, the Soviets realized that their blockade effort was futile, and finally, on May 12, 1949, the Soviet blockade of Berlin came to an end. Even after the blockade was lifted, the Berlin Airlift continued for several more months, lasting a total of fifteen, with countless planes landing in Berlin.

At the Airlift's conclusion, the American and British air forces had combined to supply Berlin with over two million tons of supplies. There were 101 deaths caused by crashes during the airlift (these became the first casualties of the Cold War). The cost of the airlift was $224 million, however most believed it was a small price to pay to secure the lives and freedom of those in West Berlin.

The Iron Curtain

The phrase Iron Curtain is frequently used in relation to the Cold War era. What exactly does this phrase mean? Why was it used?

The NATO Flag

In 1946, during a speech to Westminster College in Fulton, Missouri, former British Prime Minister Winston Churchill used the phrase "Iron Curtain" to describe the divide between Western and Eastern Europe following the end of WWII. "From Stettin in the Baltic to Trieste in the Adriatic, an iron curtain has descended across the continent."

The nations of Eastern Europe were communist dictatorships with little personal freedom granted to their citizens. People were not allowed to travel freely, and it was often difficult to get accurate information in and out of these nations.

The concept of the Iron Curtain was best defined by the rivalry between what came to be known as NATO and the Warsaw Pact states which operated under Soviet influence.

In 1949, the United States, along with the United Kingdom, France, Canada, and eight other nations, signed a treaty creating the North Atlantic Treaty Organization, also known as NATO. The member nations agreed that an armed attack against any one of them would be viewed and treated as an armed attack against all of them.

Therefore, the members pledged that if one nation was attacked by the Soviet Union, or another communist nation, that the other member nations would retaliate in an appropriate manner.

Several years later, in 1955, the Eastern European nations created the Warsaw Pact. Led by the Soviet Union, eight communist nations (including East Germany, Poland, Romania, and several others) established a mutual defense treaty.

The Red Star:

A traditional symbol for communist nations.

Although the nations of NATO never fought an actual war against the Warsaw Pact nations, the feud between the rival factions persisted for 36 years in the form of the Cold War. The Warsaw Pact officially disbanded in 1991 with the collapse of the Soviet Union.

Multiple Choice: *Please answer the following questions related to the passages you just read:*

1._____ Which nation did NOT control a portion of Germany after World War II?
a. The United States   b. Italy   c. Great Britain   d. The Soviet Union

2._____ Why did the Soviet Union halt all traffic between East and West Berlin?
a. The Soviet Union was attempting to provoke war with the United States
b. There was an outbreak of a life-threatening disease, and the Soviets were attempting to protect all those in West Berlin
c. This was in response to the decision to adopt a new currency, the Deutsche Mark
d. The citizens of East Berlin voted that they no longer wanted contact with West Berlin

3._____ What was the American and British response to the Soviet blockade of West Berlin?
a. The Berlin Airlift
b. A declaration of war
c. The surrendering of West Berlin to the Soviet Union
d. Military buildup along the border between the two halves of Germany

4._____ Why could the Soviet Union not fire on the planes flying into West Berlin?
a. Each plane was carrying a Soviet hostage
b. The planes were carrying nuclear weapons, which would explode if fired upon
c. The planes utilized stealth technology and thus, could not be seen by Soviet radar
d. Firing on the planes would have been considered an act of war

5._____ What was the significance of the Berlin Airlift?
a. It provided necessary food and supplies to the people of West Berlin during the Soviet Blockade, proving to the Soviets how far the US would go to protect West Berlin.
b. This proved to be the last major conflict between the Western Allies and the Soviet Union
c. This was the beginning of a full-scale war between the US and the Soviet Union
d. The United States realized that the Soviet Union had a far superior military and gave up all hope of defending Western Europe

6._____ Winston Churchill was the first to use which phrase to describe the relationship between Western and Eastern Europe?
a. The Great Divide   b. The Iron Curtain   c. The Iron Cross   d. The Stone Wall

7._____ What did Winston Churchill mean by the phrase used in the previous question?
a. He was referring to the iron ore deposits at the base of the Danube River
b. He was acknowledging the stone masonry traditions of the German people
c. He was referring to the political and cultural divide between Western and Eastern Europe
d. He was referencing the mountain range which separates the two halves of Europe

8._____ The initials NATO stand for?
a. North American Treaty Organization
b. National American Transit Operation
c. National Aeronautic Tactical Outpost
d. North Atlantic Treaty Organization

9._____ The Warsaw Pact nations were located where?
a. Eastern Europe   b. Western Europe   c. South America   d. Africa

10._____ Why did the Warsaw Pact disband in 1991?
a. The Warsaw Pact had defeated its enemies and was therefore no longer necessary
b. The nations of NATO defeated the Warsaw Pact in combat
c. The Soviet Union and other Warsaw Pact nations abandoned communism
d. The Warsaw Pact nations signed multiple peace treaties with the NATO nations.

Free Response Questions for the Berlin Airlift and the Iron Curtain:

1) Describe the Berlin Airlift in your own words. Do you believe that the Allied/Western response was worth the enormous cost? Why or why not?

2) Explain why you believe British Prime Minister Winston Churchill chose the words "Iron Curtain" to describe Soviet influence in Eastern Europe? Why do you think people continued using the name?

3) Why do you think the Soviet Union created the Warsaw Pact with their neighboring allies shortly after the formation of NATO? Do you feel that it was an effective strategy? Why or why not?

Cold War Vocabulary: The Berlin Airlift and the Iron Curtain

a. Blockade
b. Isolated
c. Dictatorship
d. Warsaw Pact
e. Berlin Airlift

f. Iron Curtain
g. Hostile
h. NATO
i. Necessities
j. Casualties

1._____ The effort made by the United States and its allies to provide supplies to West Berlin.

2._____ Set apart; detached from the rest.

3._____ Unfriendly; in opposition to.

4._____ Items which are required or indispensable.

5._____ The surrounding of a place with troops or naval vessels in order to prevent entrance or exit.

6._____ Members of the armed forces lost to death, wounds, sickness or capture.

7._____ The term used to describe the political and cultural divide between Eastern and Western Europe.

8._____ A nation in which all of the power is held by one individual.

9._____ An alliance formed by the United States and many Western European nations to assist each other with defense.

10._____ An alliance formed by the Soviet Union and the Eastern European nations to assist each other with defense.

Cold War Vocabulary: Fill in the Blank
Use the words from the word bank, and write in the correct choice to complete the sentence.

a. Blockade
b. Isolated
c. Dictatorship
d. Warsaw Pact
e. Berlin Airlift

f. Iron Curtain
g. Hostile
h. NATO
i. Necessities
j. Casualties

1. The United States and its allies provided _____ to the people of West Berlin during the Soviet blockade.

2. Many of the Eastern European nations were communist and under the rule of a _____ with little personal freedom.

3. West Berlin was located in the middle of the _____ territory of East Germany.

4. The members of _____ agreed that an attack against one of them would be considered an attack against all of them.

5. The Soviet Union established a _____ around West Berlin, stopping all traffic which led into and out of the city.

6. The United States and Great Britain were able to defeat the Soviet blockade through an extensive effort known as the _____.

7. West Berlin was completely _____ deep inside the hostile territory of East Germany.

8. Those who died during the Berlin Airlift became the first _____ of the Cold War.

9. The Soviet Union and its allies formed the _____ as an answer to NATO.

10. In 1946, Winston Churchill said that an _____ had descended across the continent of Europe.

The Truman Doctrine

In March of 1947, President Harry Truman delivered a speech regarding the potential fate of two nations, Greece and Turkey. Both countries were experiencing economic and political turmoil, and Truman concluded that the US should do everything within its power to assist these nations. He feared that if Greece and Turkey were left to their own accord, they would become communist nations.

Truman believed communism must be halted and not allowed to spread to other nations. Many feel that this speech was the beginning of what became known as the Cold War. It effectively established the Truman Doctrine as America's policy towards communism.

Harry Truman

The Truman Doctrine was a policy of containment. This suggested that the US would not try to eliminate communism, but instead, simply confine it to the nations where communism already existed. The reason for the containment policy was known as the Domino Theory. Foreign policy experts believed that if one nation in a region fell to communism, nearby nations could fall as well, similar to dominoes falling upon each other.

Financial aid to Greece and Turkey was one of the first actions of the Truman Doctrine policy. The two nations were given more than $400 million to help rebuild their economy and firmly establish their government. However, this was just the beginning.

In 1948, the US began assisting other nations in Western Europe. The Marshall Plan (named after Secretary of State George Marshall) was a monetary assistance program. Over the course of four years, the nations of Western Europe were given more than $12 billion to aid in rebuilding after the widespread destruction of World War II. This was done in the hopes that it would help these nations resist communism and prevent them from falling under the influence of the Soviet Union.

George Marshall

The Truman Doctrine and the policy of containment were also responsible for the US entry into multiple military conflicts throughout the 1950s, '60s, '70s, and '80s. The most prominent being the Korean Conflict and the Vietnam Conflict. In both cases, the US was attempting to prevent the spread of communism. This effort proved successful for South Korea, but it failed in Vietnam.

Containment continued to be one of the dominant forms of dealing with the communist threat throughout the remainder of the Cold War.

Multiple Choice: *Please answer the following questions related to the passage you just read:*

1._____ America's policy towards communism through much of the Cold War was known as?

a. The Marshall Plan
b. The Truman Doctrine
c. The Monroe Doctrine
d. The Roosevelt Corollary

2._____ The policy of 'containment' was an effort to contain what?

a. They were attempting to contain a dangerous disease which had affected several countries in Asia.
b. They were attempting to contain a radiation leak which threatened to contaminate several rivers.
c. They were attempting to contain communism and prevent it from spreading to other nations.
d. They were attempting to contain a flood, which was preparing to engulf several major cities.

3._____ If one nation fell to communism, other nations in the same region would also fall. This theory was known as?

a. The Slippery Slope Theory
b. The Chain Reaction Theory
c. The Avalanche Theory
d. The Domino Theory

4._____ What was the Marshall Plan?

a. An assistance program to help the nations of Western Europe rebuild
b. An invasion plan created for a possible attack on the Soviet Union
c. A plan designed to help poor American families purchase new homes
d. A plan which would help citizens respond in the event of a nuclear attack

5._____ Which two major military conflicts resulted because of the containment policy?

a. World War I & World War II
b. World War II & Korean Conflict
c. Korean Conflict & Vietnam Conflict
d. Vietnam Conflict & Gulf War

Free Response Questions for the Truman Doctrine and the Marshall Plan:

1) Describe President Truman's plan for halting the spread of communism. Do you feel that such a policy could be effective? Why or why not?

2) Why did the United States give economic aid to several Western European nations? Do you believe the act of good will was something the United States should have done? Explain your answer.

3) What military conflicts did the United States get involved in due to the policy of containment? Do you think the United States should have been willing to commit troops and suffer battlefield deaths to prevent communism from spreading? Justify your answer.

Cold War Vocabulary: The Truman Doctrine and the Marshall Plan

a. Dominant   f. Prominent
b. Harry Truman   g. The Marshall Plan
c. Monetary   h. Truman Doctrine
d. Turmoil   i. Domino Theory
e. Containment   j. Implemented

1._____ The American President through the early stages of the Cold War in the late 1940s.

2._____ The United States' policy of containment throughout most of the Cold War.

3._____ This approach suggested that the US would not try to eliminate communism, but confine it to nations where it already existed.

4._____ A theory that suggested if one nation fell to communism, others nearby could also fall.

5._____ An assistance program to help rebuild Western Europe.

6._____ Having been put into effect through a definite plan.

7._____ Pertaining to currency or money.

8._____ A leader; important or well-known.

9._____ Ruling, governing, or controlling.

10._____ A state of great commotion, confusion or disturbance.

Cold War Vocabulary: Fill in the Blank
Use the words from the word bank, and write in the correct choice to complete the sentence.

a. Dominant
b. Harry Truman
c. Monetary
d. Turmoil
e. Containment

f. Prominent
g. The Marshall Plan
h. Truman Doctrine
i. Domino Theory
j. Implemented

1. Communism was the _____ form of government throughout much of Eastern Europe and Southeast Asia during the Cold War.

2. President Truman's speech in 1947 established the _____ as the United States official policy towards communism.

3. It was hoped that rebuilding Western Europe through _____ would prevent those nations from becoming communist.

4. Many people believed that containment was necessary to prevent other nations from falling to communism because of the _____.

5. The policy of containment was established by this American President _____.

6. The financial aid to Greece and Turkey was one of the first plans _____ under the Truman Doctrine.

7. The Marshall Plan was a _____ assistance plan to help the nations of Western Europe rebuild after World War II.

8. President Truman believed that Greece and Turkey needed assistance, because the two nations were experiencing economic and political _____.

9. The Truman Doctrine was a policy of _____.

10. Two _____ examples of the US practicing containment in Southeast Asia were the Korean Conflict and the Vietnam Conflict.

Chinese Civil War

China has been a communist nation since 1949. But, how did they become communist?

Starting in 1927, China began fighting a civil war. The war pitted the forces of the Chinese Nationalist Party against the Red Army of the Chinese Communist Party. As the war progressed, the eventual leaders of this conflict were Chiang Kai-Shek (who led the Nationalists) and Mao Tse Tung (leader of the Communists).

Mao Tse Tung gained prominence in the Red Army because of an event known as the Long March. The Long March occurred in 1934 at a point when the Nationalists appeared to be on the verge of victory. As the Red Army retreated, they evaded Chiang Kai-Shek's forces for 370 days and traveled more than 8,000 miles.

Mao Tse Tung

His leadership during the Long March established Mao as the commander of the communist forces. But the war was not over. The two sides would continue fighting for many years.

In 1937, the Chinese Civil War was put on hold when Japan invaded China. At that point, the Chinese Nationalists and the Red Army joined forces with the intent of driving out the Japanese. This war against Japan became known as the Second Sino-Japanese War. The war lasted for eight years and eventually became a part of World War II as the Allied Nations (the United States, Great Britain, etc.) assisted the Chinese in defeating Japan.

However, even throughout the Sino-Japanese War, the two Chinese factions continued planning to attack one another once the Japanese were driven from their country. In 1945, at the conclusion of that war, the Chinese Civil War resumed.

The fighting continued for another four years, with the Red Army of Mao Tse Tung eventually defeating Chiang Kai-Shek's Chinese Nationalists. The Nationalists fled and established the island nation of Taiwan (which, to this day, is officially known as the Republic of China).

Chiang Kai-Shek

Meanwhile, the nation of China was taken over by the Red Army, with Mao Tse Tung becoming the Chairman of the Communist Party (he became known by most as Chairman Mao). The nation of China was renamed The People's Republic of China and officially became a communist nation.

To this day, there has never been a peace treaty signed between the two factions, therefore, the war has never officially ended. The People's Republic of China still claims ownership over the island of Taiwan, while The Republic of China (Taiwan) claims to be the legitimate government of mainland China.

The Korean Conflict

The United States and the Soviet Union never fought each other directly during the Cold War. However, there were multiple wars in which the two countries assisted opposing nations. One of those wars was the Korean Conflict. So, what was the Korean Conflict, and who was involved?

At the conclusion of World War II, in 1945, the nation of Korea, which had been controlled by Japan during the war, was divided into two pieces along the 38th parallel (referring to the latitude). North Korea was administered by the Soviet Union, while South Korea was governed by the United States.

The Soviet Union assisted North Korea in establishing a Communist government, led by Kim Il Sung, while the United States helped South Korea create a capitalist nation.

On June 25th, 1950, North Korea, with the assistance of the Soviet Union, invaded South Korea. The United States and several other nations immediately came to the assistance of South Korea. However, approximately 88% of the fighting force was supplied by the United States. The American soldiers were commanded by one of the heroes of World War II, Douglas MacArthur. In October of 1950, China entered the war as well, aiding the North Koreans.

After early difficulties, the combined forces of the US and South Korea were able to recapture Seoul (the capital of South Korea) and eventually drive the North Koreans back to the 38th parallel.

Douglas MacArthur

As the war continued, little progress was made by either side. In April of 1951, President Truman made the controversial decision to remove MacArthur from command. The decision was made for several reasons. MacArthur had provoked the Chinese into entering the war by crossing the 38th parallel. He also openly criticized President Truman's handling of the conflict, believing that he, not the President, should have the authority to use nuclear weapons.

For the next two years, the opposing sides went back and forth, with all nations involved suffering many losses. There were significant battles such as Heartbreak Ridge and Pork Chop Hill, but the end result was a prolonged stalemate, with neither side gaining a clear advantage.

After three long and bloody years, a cease fire agreement was signed between the two nations in July of 1953. A Demilitarized Zone (known as the DMZ) was established at the 38th parallel. The DMZ is a 2.5 mile wide zone between the two nations where no military personnel or equipment is allowed. The area surrounding the DMZ still remains the most heavily fortified border in the world.

At the conclusion of the Korean Conflict, the United States had suffered more than 35,000 deaths and more than 8,000 soldiers were declared "missing in action". North and South Korea combined for two million casualties.

Multiple Choice: Please answer the following questions related to the passages you just read:

1._____ Who was Mao Tse Tung?
a. He was the leader of the Chinese Communists during the Chinese Civil War
b. He was a religious leader who encouraged the Chinese to avoid war at all cost
c. He was the leader of the Chinese Nationalists during the Chinese Civil War
d. He was an influential writer who encouraged the Chinese to attack the United States

2._____ Which of the following best describes The Long March?
a. The Chinese forced prisoners to march across the Gobi Desert
b. A springtime offensive by the Chinese Nationalists, which occurred during the month of March
c. A retreat by the Chinese Communists, which lasted well over a year
d. The victorious march by the Chinese Communists as they entered Beijing

3._____ The war between China and Japan was known as?
a. The War for Chinese Liberation   c. The Indochina War
b. The War of Japanese Aggression   d. The Sino-Japanese War

4._____ The Chinese Nationalist Party eventually fled to this location.
a. Taiwan   c. Vietnam
b. Thailand   d. Japan

5._____ After taking control of the country, what did the communists officially
              rename China?
a. The Republic of China   c. The Communist Chinese Republic
b. The People's Republic of China   d. The Soviet Chinese Union

6._____ Which nation supported North Korea in its effort to become a communist nation?
a. Japan   c. The Soviet Union
b. Germany   d. Vietnam

7._____ This location was the border between North and South Korea.
a. Korea Bay   c. 38th Parallel
b. 48th Parallel   d. Sea of Japan

8._____ The leader of North Korea was?
a. Ngo Dinh Diem   c. Ho Chi Minh
b. Mao Tse Tung   d. Kim Il Sung

9._____ Why did President Harry Truman remove Douglas MacArthur from command
              in Korea?
a. General MacArthur had attempted to seize command from President Truman
b. General MacArthur was deemed to be mentally unfit for duty
c. General MacArthur was killed in action and therefore had to be replaced
d. General MacArthur had provoked the Chinese into entering the war

10._____ The heavily fortified border between North and South Korea is known as?
a. The Berlin Wall   c. The Sudetenland
b. The Demilitarized Zone   d. The Great Divide

Free Response Questions for the Chinese Civil War and the Korean Conflict:

1) Why did the opposing sides in the Chinese Civil War temporarily cease fighting one another in 1937? Why do you feel that they could not maintain the peace once their common problem was eliminated?

2) Why did President Harry Truman fire General Douglas MacArthur? Do you believe his reasons were valid? Explain your answer.

3) Compare and contrast the Korean Conflict and the Chinese Civil War. How were the similar? How were they different?

Cold War Vocabulary: The Chinese Civil War and the Korean Conflict

a. 38th Parallel
b. Kim Il Sung
c. Stalemate
d. Chiang Kai Shek
e. The Long March

f. Mao Tse Tung
g. The DMZ
h. Douglas MacArthur
i. The People's Republic of China
j. The Republic of China

1._____ Leader of the Chinese Nationalist Party during the Chinese Civil War.

2._____ Leader of the Chinese Red Army during the Chinese Civil War.

3._____ A retreat by the Red Army which lasted more than a year.

4._____ The official name given to China after the Communists seized control.

5._____ The official name given to Taiwan, after the Chinese Nationalists fled to that island.

6._____ The border separating North and South Korea.

7._____ The communist leader of North Korea.

8._____ Commander of American forces in Korea throughout most of the Korean Conflict.

9._____ A situation in which neither side is gaining a clear advantage.

10._____ A heavily-fortified region between North and South Korea where no weapons are permitted.

Cold War Vocabulary: Fill in the Blank
Use the words from the word bank, and write in the correct choice to complete the sentence.

a. 38th Parallel
b. Kim Il Sung
c. Stalemate
d. Chiang Kai Shek
e. The Long March

f. Mao Tse Tung
g. The DMZ
h. Douglas MacArthur
i. The People's Republic of China
j. The Republic of China

1. The Soviet Union assisted _____ in establishing a communist government in North Korea.

2. After three years of fighting, North and South Korea had reached a _____.

3. In 1951, President Truman made the controversial decision of removing _____ from command.

4. Mao Tse Tung gained prominence in the Red Army during _____.

5. When the Communists gained control of China, they renamed the nation _____.

6. The border between North and South Korea is separated by a heavily fortified region known as _____.

7. _____ and the Chinese Nationalist Party opposed the Communists in China.

8. The Chinese Nationalist Party fled to the island of Taiwan, where they adopted the official name of _____.

9. The border between North and South Korea was established at the _____.

10. Chinese Communists led by _____ eventually took control of China.

Cold War Spies

Spies are not just something for the movies. Sometimes, especially during the Cold War, spies were quite real. So, who were the spies? And what happened to them?

Alger Hiss

In 1948, a man named Alger Hiss was accused of being a Communist by Whittaker Chambers, a former Communist Party member. Hiss protested his innocence, claiming that he was not a Communist and that he had never even met Mr. Chambers.

But Chambers came back and said that not only was Alger Hiss a Communist, but he was a spy as well. As proof, he presented 65 pages of documents and several rolls of 35 mm film, all of which proved Hiss's ties to espionage. He had hidden this evidence inside a hollowed out pumpkin in the middle of a pumpkin patch, thus, the evidence against Hiss became known as "The Pumpkin Papers".

As the case unfolded, it was revealed that Hiss knew Mr. Chambers, had rented an apartment to him, and had even given him a car several years before. Alger Hiss was found guilty of perjury and sentenced to 44 months in prison. To his dying day, he insisted that he was innocent.

But, Alger Hiss was not the only spy convicted in the United States. There was also the case of Julius and Ethel Rosenberg.

In 1949, the Soviet Union tested their first atomic bomb. The United States was shocked that the Soviets had succeeded in developing the device as quickly as they did. After a significant amount of investigation, it was discovered that a network of spies had passed top secret information to the Soviets, which had helped them develop the bomb.

Ethel & Julius Rosenberg

Amongst the many people involved in that conspiracy were a couple named Julius and Ethel Rosenberg, members of the Communist Party in New York City. When the case went to trial, it was shown that Ethel had typed out several documents related to nuclear secrets, and Julius had turned over sketches of parts to an atomic bomb.

In March of 1951, the couple was convicted of espionage charges and both were sentenced to death. The sentence was carried out on June 19th, 1953. They were the only Americans executed for espionage during the Cold War.

The Rosenbergs and Alger Hiss represent just three of what were surely many spies who operated in both countries.

The Red Scare: Part One

Throughout the Cold War, many Americans harbored an intense fear and hatred of communism. Why were they so afraid? Where did this hatred come from?

In February of 1950, Senator Joseph McCarthy produced a list of 205 names. He claimed that all of these were people who worked within the State Department and were also Communists. Following this revelation, Senator McCarthy began a series of Congressional investigations in which countless accusations were made towards many individuals.

Joseph McCarthy

Senator McCarthy's investigations, as well as those of the House Un-American Activities Committee (HUAC), helped create the atmosphere of fear and resentment towards communists that would dominate the next two decades. Because of Senator McCarthy's efforts, the phrase "McCarthyism" was used to describe the act of accusing someone, with little or no evidence.

In the early 50s, there were also several pieces of legislation passed that increased the paranoia against communism. The best example was the Internal Security Act of 1950. This law required Communist organizations to register with the Attorney General's office. Members of these organizations were not allowed to become citizens of the US (if they already *were* they could possibly *lose* their citizenship).

There was also a "Federal Employees Loyalty Program". This was a review board that determined the "Americanism" of federal employees. The board recommended that any employee suspected of being "Un-American" should have their employment terminated. Across the nation, many states, communities, and even private businesses also established "Loyalty Review Boards". It is estimated that by the end of the 1950s around 20% of all employees had to pass some sort of loyalty review.

If an employee was discharged because they were deemed to be "disloyal" to the nation, their life could potentially be ruined. No other employer would be willing to hire someone with this type of speculation in their background. Some industries even developed "blacklists" to prevent "disloyal citizens" from being hired. "Blacklisting" is a term used to describe the informal exclusion of a certain group from employment. Blacklisting was especially prominent in high profile fields such as the entertainment industry (television and movies) and government employment.

Throughout this time period, thanks to the anticommunist hysteria, thousands of honest and loyal Americans were accused of being Communists, or communist sympathizers.

The Red Scare: Part Two

Organizations like the House Un-American Activities Committee and the Loyalty Review Boards were not the only reasons that fear of communism spread throughout the nation in the Post WWII era. So, what other factors helped to spread the fear among the American public?

Nearly all of the popular forms of media (television, radio, movies, and print) featured anti-communist propaganda in some way. Most of this content was geared towards younger audiences in an effort to raise a generation that would both despise communism and be terrified by it.

Many early television programs of the 1950s had an anti-communist theme as a regular part of their programming. Shows such as *The Man Called X* and *I Led Three Lives* featured characters who were spying communists attempting to undermine the government, or the American way of life. Radio programs like *I was Communist for the FBI* featured similar themes.

The movie industry was not to be outdone. Throughout the 1950s, there were many films made with anti-communist messages. The most well-known include; *I Married a Communist* and *The Red Menace*. Science fiction films were a popular outlet for this fear as well. Many science fiction films featured plots involving "un-American" and inhuman aliens attempting to infiltrate American society and change the way of life.

Comic books were a popular pastime for America's youth in the 1950s and '60s. Therefore, the comics were also filled with stories about spies and Communist villains. Publications such as paperback novels also commonly presented Communists in the role of villain.

I Married a Communist

The Cold War anti-communist hysteria even drifted into professional sports. The Major League Baseball team known as the Cincinnati Reds temporarily changed their mascot to the "Redlegs" in an effort to avoid a connection with communism (the term "Reds" was often used as a synonym for communists).

Multiple Choice: *Please answer the following questions related to the passages you just read:*

1._____ What was Alger Hiss accused of?
a. He was accused of smuggling illegal immigrants into the country
b. He was accused of being a communist spy
c. He was accused of attempting to lead a communist uprising in the US
d. He was accused of operating an illegal gambling operation

2._____ The man who made the accusations of Alger Hiss was?
a. Joseph McCarthy   c. Whittaker Chambers
b. Richard Nixon   d. Forrest Whitaker

3._____ The evidence which eventually helped convict Alger Hiss became known as?
a. The Pumpkin Papers   c. The Police Files
b. The Pentagon Papers   d. The Potomac Files

4._____ This couple became the only Americans to receive the death penalty for being spies.
a. Pierre & Marie Curie   c. Julius & Ethel Rosenberg
b. John & Jane Doe   d. Mike & Suzy Johnson

5._____ The couple mentioned in the previous question were accused of what?
a. They were accused of attempting to overthrow top generals in the United States
b. They were accused of attempting to assassinate the President
c. They were accused of leading a workers rebellion in a major factory
d. They were accused of passing secrets regarding the atomic bomb

6._____ What is the significance of Senator Joseph McCarthy?
a. In the early 1950s, he began accusing many different people of being communist
b. He was accused of being a Soviet spy and given a life sentence in prison
c. He replaced Douglas MacArthur as the new commander in Korea
d. He developed the hydrogen bomb, which became an important weapon throughout the Cold War.

7._____ What did the initials HUAC stand for?
a. Housing & Urban Access Committee
b. Hispanic Unified Artists Coalition
c. House Unethical Activities Committee
d. House Un-American Activities Committee

8._____ According to the Internal Security Act of 1950, what could happen to a person who was discovered to be a communist?
a. The person would be executed
b. The person would not be allowed to become a citizen
c. The person would be put on display in the town square as a known communist
d. The person would no longer be allowed to vote

9._____ If the Loyalty Review Board found someone to be "Un-American", what might the consequence be?
a. The person's position would be terminated
b. The person would be immediately deported
c. The person would be placed in a re-education center'.
d. The person would be forced to undergo a series of psychological examinations

10._____ When someone is informally excluded from holding certain jobs, this is known as what?
a. Roughnecking
b. Bricklaying
c. Tripchecking
d. Blacklisting

11._____ Some television and radio programs were used for what purpose in the 1950s?
a. To pass secret messages to the Soviets
b. To influence young adults into joining the military
c. To promote anti-communist propaganda
d. To promote vegetarianism in the general public

12._____ Which of these is an example of a movie that presented an anti-communist message?
a. *Rebel Without a Cause*
b. *The Red Menace*
c. *West Side Story*
d. *A Streetcar Named Desire*

13._____ What genre of films were frequently used to help spread the fear of things that were deemed to be "un-American"?
a. Horror
b. Comedies
c. Dramas
d. Science Fiction

14._____ Aside from comic books, what other type of publication frequently featured communist villains?
a. Biographies
b. Periodicals
c. Professional Journals
d. Paperback Novels

15._____ Why did the Cincinnati Reds change their mascot to the Redlegs during the 1950s?
a. The term "Reds" was used as a nickname for communists
b. It was discovered that another professional team already used that nickname
c. The owner of the franchise disliked the original mascot
d. The term "Reds" was deemed offensive to certain minority groups

Free Response Questions for Cold War Spies and the Red Scare

1) Explain why you believe the nation had such a strong fear of communism in the Post WWII era. Do you feel that such a reaction to the threat of communism was justified? Why or why not?

2) Why do you feel that the punishment for Ethel and Julius Rosenberg was so severe? Do you believe that such punishments are ever warranted (justified)? Support your answer.

3) Create your own movie title for a Cold War era film and give a brief description of the movie plot in the space provided below. What would the movie poster look like?

Cold War Vocabulary: Cold War Spies and the Red Scare

a. Propaganda
b. McCarthyism
c. Espionage
d. Hysteria
e. Joseph McCarthy

f. Reds
g. Blacklist
h. HUAC
i. Infiltrate
j. Paranoia

1._____ US Senator who was largely responsible for generating the fear of communism in the Early 1950s.

2._____ A committee in the House of Representatives which helped create the atmosphere of fear towards communists.

3._____ To pass a small number into a territory with subversive intent.

4._____ The informal exclusion of a certain group from employment.

5._____ The act of accusing someone with little or no evidence.

6._____ Information, ideas, or rumors deliberately spread to help or harm a person, group, or nation.

7._____ A nickname given to communists.

8._____ An uncontrolled outburst of emotion, usually fear, characterized by irrational behavior.

9._____ An intense fear or suspicion, usually without reason.

10._____ The act or practice of spying.

Name_____

Cold War Vocabulary: Fill in the Blank
Use the words from the word bank, and write in the correct choice to complete the sentence.

a. Propaganda
b. McCarthyism
c. Espionage
d. Hysteria
e. Joseph McCarthy

f. Reds
g. Blacklist
h. HUAC
i. Infiltrate
j. Paranoia

1. During the Red Scare era, the US government convicted Ethel and Julius Rosenberg of _____.

2. Senator _____ claimed that 205 communists were working in the State Department.

3. Many movies in the 1950s suggested that communists were attempting to _____ American society and change our way of life.

4. The tactics used by Joseph McCarthy gave rise to the phrase _____.

5. Many actors were placed on a _____, which prevented them from working in the entertainment industry.

6. The anti-communist _____ during the Cold War led people to do many irrational things.

7. Many citizens were brought before _____, a House of Representatives committee which investigated communists.

8. Television, radio, and movies were all used to spread anti-communist _____.

9. Throughout the 1950s the _____, or intense fear, of communism persisted.

10. The nickname _____ was used for communists, which led to the term "Red Scare" to describe the era.

Reading Through History   31 | P a g e

Civil Defense at School

During the height of the Cold War, there were many drills, routines, film strips and pamphlets designed to help citizens survive a nuclear attack. What were some of these things, and who designed them?

Children "ducking and covering"

during an air raid drill.

President Harry Truman created the Federal Civil Defense Administration (FCDA) in 1950 in an effort to help the nation prepare for the possibility of a nuclear attack. The FCDA did many things throughout the 1950s and '60s to help people maintain a level of awareness.

There were many efforts undertaken, largely focusing on schools and educating children about proper procedures. Home Economics classes taught girls what items should be included in a fallout shelter. Comic books were even created and distributed to school children that promoted nuclear safety.

Probably the most famous effort to educate children came through the use of "Bert the Turtle". Bert was an animated turtle who appeared in film strips promoting the "duck and cover" safety strategy. Bert instructed that, in the event of a nuclear attack, first, one was supposed to "duck" out of the way to protect from flying debris and then "cover" your head and body to prevent burns and serious cuts. The films were accompanied by a catchy song that many could still sing years later.

Schools took other measures as well. Many districts began practicing weekly air raid drills that utilized a similar "duck and cover" method. When the students heard the warning siren, they were instructed to hide under their desks to protect their heads from falling objects.

Other school districts took even more extreme measures. Some went as far as purchasing identification bracelets for all of their students. This was to make it easier to identify victims in case of a major attack.

These precautions and many others serve as a reminder of just how frightening it might have been to have lived during the Cold War era.

Civil Defense at Home

Schools were not the only place where the Federal Civil Defense Administration was attempting to make people safe. Outside of school, they were also trying to help the general population understand what steps they could take to be safer. How did the FCDA try to accomplish this task?

There were many different steps taken by the FCDA. Brochures, films and radio segments all focused on "what to do" in the event of a nuclear attack. The FCDA also distributed millions of instruction manuals and handbooks, such as "How to Survive an Atomic Bomb". Most of these manuals were optimistic in nature and stressed that the most important thing was "to stay calm and not panic".

The FCDA encouraged women to take the lead in civil defense in many different ways. Women were taught that good housekeeping was one of the first steps in preventing fires. They also received tips on how to stock a first aid kit and medical tags, how to prepare a shelter in a basement, and how to recognize the different types of air raid sirens.

The FCDA even began a program known as "Grandma's Pantry" in which it was recommended that all homes keep a supply of at least two weeks of non-perishable food in their pantry. The name of the program was to remind everyone of a simpler time when "Grandma always had enough food in her house to protect the family from any natural disaster."

Women also frequently served as "block wardens" throughout the 1950s and '60s. A block warden was supposed to organize families (usually about 25 to 30 families), so that the neighborhood would have a coordinated plan in case of an attack.
The FCDA often referred to block wardens as "the backbone of civil defense".

Aside from block wardens, there were other volunteer positions as well, such as fire wardens, rescue wardens, first aid wardens, evacuation wardens, and communications wardens. Some citizens also volunteered for the important position of "spotter" for the US Air Force. These were civilians who were trained to watch the skies and keep an eye out for enemy aircraft.

These and many other measures helped the average citizen feel more secure during the troubled times of the Cold War era.

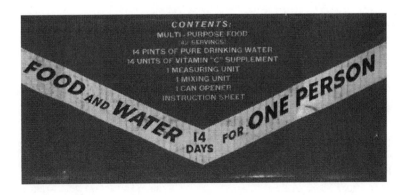

Multiple Choice: *Please answer the following questions related to the passages you just read:*

1._____ To help the nation prepare for the threats created by the Soviet Union, President Harry Truman created this organization in 1950.
a. Federal Civil Defense Administration
b. House Un-American Activities Committee
c. Federal Emergency Management Authority
d. Civil Defense and Emergency Management Agency

2._____ What were girls taught about civil defense in Home Economics class?
a. They were taught the proper procedure of how to load firearms
b. They were taught what items should be included in a fallout shelter
c. They were taught how to organize a community civil defense strategy
d. They were taught how to decontaminate radioactive surfaces

3._____ What was the name of the animated character that taught students about nuclear safety?
a. Bugs Bunny   c. Smilin' Joe Fusion
b. Tommy the Atom   d. Bert the Turtle

4._____ This was the safety strategy taught by the character mentioned in the previous question.
a. Catch and Release   c. Duck and Cover
b. Stop, Drop, and Roll   d. Drop and Flatten

5._____ Where were children instructed to hide during an air raid drill?
a. In a closet   c. In the restroom
b. Under their desks   d. In the frame of a doorway

6._____ Which of these is most likely to have been a pamphlet published by the Federal Civil Defense Administration?
a. Atomic Attacks: Who to blame and why
b. Communism: Wave of the Future
c. How to Survive an Atomic Bomb
d. How to Build an Atomic Bomb

7._____ Families were encouraged to keep a food supply that would last them for how long?
a. Two weeks   c. One year
b. Five days   d. One Month

8._____ During the 1950s, women frequently served in what position?
a. Top ranking military generals
b. Director of the FCDA
c. Local Block Wardens
d. Ambassadors to communist nations

9._____ A block warden's main function was to do what?
a. Watch the skies for enemy aircraft
b. Organize social gatherings and cookouts
c. Patrol the neighborhoods each night
d. Organize families in case of an attack

10._____ What was the job of a spotter?
a. To check for suspicious vehicles in the neighborhood
b. To investigate new families that had just moved to the community
c. To watch the skies for enemy aircraft
d. To paint a black spot on all locations deemed safe during an air raid

Free Response Questions for Civil Defense at School and Home

1) Do you feel that government agencies such as the Federal Civil Defense Administration were necessary during the Cold War? Why or why not?

2) Why do you feel that the FCDA used cartoons and characters such as Bert the Turtle to relay civil defense messages to school children? Do you feel that it was a proper strategy? Support your answer.

3) Do you believe that the Federal Civil Defense Administration's approach of encouraging women to have a first aid kit and a shelter prepared in the basement was a good policy? In what other types of situations might such precautions save lives?

Cold War Vocabulary: Civil Defense at school and home

a. Block Warden
b. Precautions
c. Debris
d. Civil Defense
e. Non-perishable

f. Procedures
g. Duck and Cover
h. Coordinate
i. Brochure
j. Pantry

1._____   Plans or activities organized by civilians to prepare for times of emergency or war.

2._____   A room or storage area where food and other provisions are kept.

3._____   To organize.

4._____   A series of instructions to be followed while performing a task.

5._____   Food items which will not spoil quickly.

6._____   A short booklet containing summarized or introductory information.

7._____   An individual responsible for organizing neighborhood families in case of emergencies.

8._____   The fragments or remains of something that has been destroyed.

9._____   Measures taken in advance to secure good results.

10._____   A safety strategy that was taught in order to help protect citizens from a nuclear explosion.

Cold War Vocabulary: Fill in the Blank
Use the words from the word bank, and write in the correct choice to complete the sentence.

a. Block Warden
b. Precautions
c. Debris
d. Civil Defense
e. Non-perishable

f. Procedures
g. Duck and Cover
h. Coordinate
i. Brochure
j. Pantry

1. In school, many children were taught the _____ drill.

2. Those living during the Cold War era took many _____ to help ensure the safety of their families.

3. Block Wardens were supposed to _____ a plan of action, in case of an attack.

4. The federal government encouraged women to take the lead in _____.

5. One of the greatest dangers of an attack would be the falling _____ from destroyed buildings or objects.

6. Schools educated students in the proper _____ which should be taken in case of a nuclear attack.

7. It was recommended that all homes keep at least a two week supply of food in their _____.

8. The food items citizens were instructed to store in their pantries were supposed to be _____.

9. Many women served as their neighborhood's _____.

10. The federal government released many _____ and films which focused on what should be done during a nuclear attack.

Fallout Shelters

In the 1950s and '60s, many communities began building fallout shelters to protect residents from the threat of nuclear weapons. So, what exactly is fallout, and what did these shelters include?

Fallout is created when a nuclear explosion vaporizes objects close to the detonation, turning the objects into a very fine ash. The ash absorbs the radiation generated by the explosion and becomes radioactive. This ash, now called fallout, then drifts back to the Earth and covers everything in the area with a fine layer of radioactive dust, which is harmful to humans, animals, and plant life.

A fallout shelter was an enclosed space designed to allow its occupants to minimize exposure to the harmful fallout until the levels of radiation had dropped to a safe level. Throughout the 1950s and '60s, many communities constructed and maintained fallout shelters large enough to accommodate thousands of residents. Even major businesses began constructing shelters so that their employees could remain safe in the event of a nuclear attack.

In most cases, existing buildings with large basements made of thick concrete would be designated as public fallout shelters. Public shelters were identified by the well-known yellow and black trefoil symbol.

Shelters would usually be supplied with food and large amounts of water, sanitation supplies, and radiation detection equipment such as Geiger counters. Water was stored in 17.5 gallon metal containers, and food came in various forms, usually non-perishable in nature.

Fallout water containers

The Federal Civil Defense Administration recommended that, in the event of an attack, those inside the shelter should remain there for at least two weeks. At the end of the first week, they would be able to go outside for up to an hour at a time. As the days progressed, they could gradually increase the amount of time spent outside the shelter. While outside, the shelter residents would utilize their time sweeping, scrubbing, and washing the fallout off of roads, sidewalks, and other surfaces.

Today, all public shelters have long since been abandoned and are no longer maintained with fresh supplies. Some have even been converted to museums and serve as a reminder of what the Cold War was really like.

Family Fallout Shelters

Many communities were building large public fallout shelters intended for thousands of people. But what if a public shelter wasn't nearby or became overcrowded? Were there any steps individual families could take to protect themselves from nuclear fallout?

Throughout the 1950s and '60s, many families constructed personal fallout shelters in their backyards. Companies marketed several different "family models" for homeowners hoping to protect their families. These ranged from a $13.50 "foxhole kit" all the way up to the $5,000 "deluxe model" which featured beds, a phone, toilet, and a Geiger counter for detecting radiation levels.

Many families constructed their shelters in the middle of the night in an effort to conceal the facility from their neighbors. They feared that neighbors, who did not have shelters, would swarm their property in an emergency if they knew a shelter was there.

Some families could not afford the commercially-produced shelters, so there were a number of do-it-yourself methods for shelter construction. One popular method was to take an existing basement and reinforce it for fallout shelter purposes. Many military surplus stores sold air filters, flashlights, fallout protections suits, first aid kits, and water which people used to supply their personal shelters.

Civil Defense films encouraged the public to maintain a two week supply of water and non-perishable food in their basements. They also recommended having a battery-powered radio tuned to one of the two Civil Defense CONELRAD stations: 640 or 1240 on the AM dial.

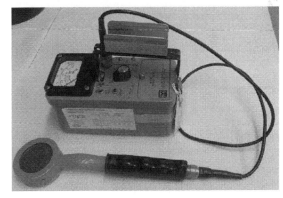

A Geiger Counter

Today, most personal fallout shelters have been removed or dismantled, but some might still be found in homes around the nation. However, most of the few that remain have almost certainly been converted into basements, or storage facilities, and only serve as a lingering reminder of the Cold War.

Effects of Nuclear Weapons

Throughout the Cold War, the threat of nuclear war was always looming. Why were these weapons thought to be so dangerous? And what were the effects of such devices?

When a nuclear device detonates, there are many ways that it can damage the human body. There are three major threats that one must worry about: heat, blast, and radiation.

First, those close to the detonation would stand no chance of survival. At the center of a nuclear explosion, the temperature can reach millions of degrees, enough to incinerate or vaporize anything within several miles. The heat is intense enough to melt rocks and metal railroad ties.

As one moves further away from the atomic blast, chance of survival becomes better, but still slim. The heat produced by the blast is so intense that fatal third degree burns can be caused up to 25 miles away.

Accompanied with this intense heat is the second threat of a nuclear explosion, a tremendous blast of air pressure. This blast can produce winds in excess of a thousand miles per hour. Buildings can instantly be leveled by this massive current, causing even more fatalities and many injuries. The blast could also be fatal through the shattering of glass and other debris.

The third danger from a nuclear explosion comes from radiation. Radiation is a form of energy which is harmful to living cells. It causes many different ailments. The more immediate effects could include nausea, vomiting, and severe headaches. Long term effects could result in a number of different physical symptoms, from hair and teeth falling out, to various forms of cancer. The effects of radiation could be even more far reaching, causing birth defects and deformities in future generations.

These are just some of the effects the detonation of a nuclear device would have on the human population of a region. It should also be noted that the plant and animal life of the area would be affected in similar ways as well. Needless to say, these devices are a weapon that most people hope will never be used again.

Multiple Choice: Please answer the following questions related to the passages you just read:

1._____ The radioactive ash created by a nuclear explosion is known as what?
a. Toxic Waste
b. Fallout
c. Nuclear Ash
d. Radiated Debris

2._____ What feature would help a building be designated as a fallout shelter?
a. High ceilings and a balcony
b. A walk-in safe and very few windows
c. Carpet flooring and large restrooms
d. Large basements with thick concrete walls

3._____ Fallout shelters were supposed to be stocked with what types of items?
a. Food, large amounts of water, and sanitation supplies
b. Plants, seed, and gardening tools to plant non-radioactive vegetables
c. Oxygen and proper gas masks to help shelter residents survive the fallout
d. Radiation suits and other protective gear to help with survival

4._____ The Federal Civil Defense Administration recommended staying in a fallout shelter for how long?
a. One year
b. Six months
c. Two weeks
d. Over night

5._____ Once you could leave the fallout shelter, the FCDA recommended that what type of activities be performed?
a. Exercise to keep in shape; play for the children
b. Scrubbing the fallout from exposed surfaces
c. A cookout to celebrate the continuation of life
d. Immediate rebuilding of damaged structures

6._____ Which types of items might be included in the "Deluxe" model fallout shelter?
a. A television and an extra-large bathtub
b. A video game system and carpeted floors
c. A phone, beds, toilet and a Geiger counter
d. A decontamination unit, which insured safety

7._____ Why did some families build their fallout shelters in the middle of the night?
a. The soil was easier to dig during the night
b. It was less expensive to hire a night time work crew
c. They feared that the communists might be spying on them
d. They did not want their neighbors to know they had a shelter

8._____ What types of supplies might be found in a military surplus store?
a. Air filters, flashlights, protective suits and first-aid kits
b. Designer clothes and fashionable shoes
c. Board games and other items to help pass the time
d. Safety manuals and survival instructions

9._____ The public was encouraged to keep a two week supply of what?
a. Clean clothing
b. Food and water
c. Coal or wood for heat
d. Books and Newspapers

10._____ What was the significance of the two radio stations 640 and 1240 AM?
a. Those stations were well-known for broadcasting baseball games
b. Those stations were dedicated to broadcasting anti-communist propaganda
c. Those stations were the civil defense stations, which would broadcast important information in the event of an attack
d. Those stations were the only stations allowed to broadcast a Presidential address

11._____ What are the three major threats of a nuclear detonation?
a. A blinding light, a flash freeze, and an earthquake
b. Throbbing in the ears, a splitting headache, and high fever
c. Eternal darkness, nuclear winter, and an earthquake
d. Heat, a tremendous blast, and radiation

12._____ Which of these best describes what would happen to someone who was near the center of a nuclear blast?
a. Most of the destructive force would go over and away from them, making the center of the blast the safest place to be
b. The person would suffer severe burns to much of their body, but would probably survive
c. The person would be instantly vaporized
d. The extreme levels of radiation would cause severe mutations, with unpredictable results

13._____ Which of these is the best estimate for how strong the blast of air pressure might be during a nuclear explosion?
a. Winds can be in excess of 1,000 miles per hour
b. Winds can be in excess of 100,000 miles per hour
c. Winds can reach approximately 300 miles per hour
d. Winds will be virtually non-existent

14._____ Which of these best describes the immediate effects that radiation might have on the body?
a. Fever, sore throat and runny nose
b. Aching back, sore muscles, and a slight rash
c. Severe acne, bad breath, and itchy scalp
d. Nausea, vomiting, and severe headaches

15._____ Which of these might be a long-term effect of exposure to high radiation?
a. Hair and tooth loss
b. Various forms of cancer
c. Birth defects in future generations
d. All of the above

Free Response Questions for Fallout Shelters and Effects of Nuclear Weapons:

1) Do you know of an area near your home that was designated as a fallout shelter? Can you describe the facility? If not, describe a nearby building that could possibly serve as a fallout shelter and explain why you would choose it.

2) Do you think you could survive two weeks confined in a fallout shelter or basement? Is there anything you believe you COULD NOT live without? What would you have to have with you and why?

3) Considering the deadly impact nuclear weapons have on civilian populations, do you feel that a country could ever be justified in using one of them again? Explain why or why not.

Cold War Vocabulary: Fallout Shelters and Effects of Nuclear Weapons

a. Fallout Shelter   f. Radiation
b. Dismantled   g. Fallout
c. Designated   h. Foxhole
d. CONELRAD   i. Surplus
e. Geiger Counter   j. Accommodate

1._____ The radioactive ash that drifts back to Earth after a nuclear explosion.

2._____ Civil defense radio stations which would have provided information in the event of a major crisis.

3._____ To supply or provide for.

4._____ A device used to measure radiation levels.

5._____ A form of energy harmful to living cells.

6._____ An enclosed space designed to minimize exposure to fallout.

7._____ To be pulled down or taken apart.

8._____ An excess of product; greater than the amount needed.

9._____ A small pit dug as shelter, usually big enough for one or two soldiers.

10._____ Selected for a specific purpose or duty.

Cold War Vocabulary: Fill in the Blank
Use the words from the word bank, and write in the correct choice to complete the sentence.

a. Fallout Shelter
b. Dismantled
c. Designated
d. CONELRAD
e. Geiger Counter

f. Radiation
g. Fallout
h. Foxhole
i. Surplus
j. Accommodate

1. The _____ radio stations could be found at 640 and 1240 on the AM dial.

2. Many families and communities built shelters to help protect them from _____, the fine radioactive ash that fell after a nuclear explosion.

3. Some fallout shelters were large enough to _____ thousands of people.

4. The "deluxe model" fallout shelter came with a _____ which was used to measure radiation levels.

5. Buildings with large concrete basements were _____ as fallout shelters.

6. Many people could not afford a factory-made _____ so they constructed their own in a basement.

7. For those who could not afford a fallout shelter, they might try to purchase a _____ kit for $13.50.

8. Military _____ stores sold air filters, flashlights, and other survival gear that might have come in useful during a nuclear attack.

9. The three biggest dangers from a nuclear explosion are the heat, blast, and _____.

10. In the modern world, most fallout shelters have been _____.

The Kitchen Debate

In July of 1959, the Vice President of the United States, Richard Nixon, visited the Soviet Union. This visit represented the first time that high ranking officials from the US and the USSR had met since 1955.

While in the Soviet Union, Nixon toured the American National Exhibition which had just opened. As part of the exhibition, a model home had been constructed, which displayed many of the modern conveniences available in the United States, such as dishwashers and washing machines.

As Vice President Nixon toured the home with Soviet Premier Nikita Khrushchev, the two leaders debated with one another over the industrial accomplishments of the two nations. As they reached the kitchen, the debate became heated. Khrushchev argued that his own nation focused on necessities, while the United States was obsessed with luxuries. While viewing the many labor-saving devices, he sarcastically asked the Vice President, "Do your people also have a machine that opens their mouth and chews for them?"

Eventually, the two leaders agreed that their nations needed to do a better job of cooperating with one another. This exchange between Nixon and Khrushchev became known as the Kitchen Debate, and it earned Nixon a large amount of respect with the American public who saw him as standing up for American ideals and principles.

During his visit to Moscow, Vice President Nixon invited Premier Khrushchev to the United States. Khrushchev accepted this invitation and, in September of 1959, became the first Premier of the Soviet Union to visit the US.

While in the United States, Premier Khrushchev visited many different locations, including Los Angeles, San Francisco, a farm in Iowa, the city of Pittsburgh, and Washington DC. The Premier concluded his trip to the US by meeting President Dwight Eisenhower at the President's private vacation resort of Camp David.

The Eisenhowers and Khrushchevs

At the conclusion of his thirteen day visit, Premier Khrushchev felt he had developed a strong relationship with President Eisenhower and was certain he could achieve peaceful cooperation with the United States. It seemed, at least for the moment, that the icy relations between the US and the Soviet Union were beginning to thaw.

The U-2

In the late 1950s, it seemed as if the Cold War was beginning to thaw out some. President Dwight Eisenhower and Soviet Premier Nikita Khrushchev had a good relationship with each other, and the two nations seemed to be cooperating.

Unfortunately, the peace would not last. In 1960, an American U-2 plane was shot down over Soviet air space. So, what kind of plane was the U-2? What did the United States use it for?

In the mid-1950s, the US Government saw the need for a new type of aircraft; a spy plane capable of flying high above the Soviet Union for the purposes of photographing bases and installations in order to monitor Soviet military strength.

Lockheed, one of the United States' top manufacturers of aircraft, was contracted to build the planes. The end result of their efforts was the "Utility Plane 2", or the "U-2" for short. The plane was capable of flying at altitudes up to fourteen miles high and could stay in the air up to eleven hours. High-powered cameras on the aircraft could photograph a golf ball placed on a putting green 14 miles below.

The pilots who flew the U-2 were required to wear a pressurized suit during flights because of the altitude and could not drink any liquids for several hours prior to each flight (the flights usually lasted seven to eight hours).

U-2 designer Kelly Johnson

with pilot Gary Powers

The U-2 made its first flight in 1957 and worked precisely as it was built to. As a result of the flights, the United States discovered that the Soviet military was not nearly as large or powerful as they were making the rest of the world believe.

But, in April of 1960, a U-2 piloted by Gary Powers was making a routine flight over the Soviet Union when the plane was struck by a Soviet missile. Powers parachuted safely to the ground, but was captured by the Soviet military. The incident provided proof of what the Soviets had been claiming for some time. The United States had been spying on the USSR.

With this discovery, the American-Soviet relationship was shattered. Because of the U-2 incident, the Cold War divide deepened even further, and it would be another 25 years before the tension softened again and any real progress would be made between the two nations.

The Berlin Wall

The Berlin Wall was one of the most intimidating symbols of the Cold War era. Who built the Berlin Wall? Why did they build it?

At the conclusion of World War II, Germany was divided into two separate nations, East Germany and West Germany. The western portion was assisted by the United States and the United Kingdom, whereas, the eastern portion was assisted by the Soviet Union. Berlin, the capital city, was also divided into West and East Berlin, in a similar fashion.

For the first several years that the two nations existed, people were allowed to travel in between the two sides. However, as time progressed and conditions worsened in communist East Germany, many people began escaping to the Western side.

The East Germans were determined to put an end to these defections. In August of 1961, the East Germans ordered that the border between East and West Germany be closed. This included cutting the city of Berlin in half and erecting a border between the two. East German soldiers began demolishing the streets between the two halves and established a temporary barbwire fence.

With the splitting of Berlin, many lives were thrown into chaos. Families were no longer able to visit their relatives, and in some cases, East Berliners were cut off from their jobs on the West Berlin side.

The East Germans then erected a permanent wall made of concrete, which came to be known as the Berlin Wall. The wall was an 87-mile-long fortified structure featuring 116 watch towers, dogs, additional chain link fences, barbwire, and trenches to prevent vehicles from driving across. It also included a secondary wall on the East Berlin side. The space between the two walls became known as "the Death Strip" as East German guards were instructed to shoot anyone attempting to escape.

The border between the two halves of Berlin wasn't completely closed, however. There were several checkpoints where visitors could pass into East Berlin (although, very few East Berliners were allowed to travel into West Berlin). The most well-known of these crossings was "Checkpoint Charlie", and it was the only crossing where Americans and many other foreigners were allowed to pass.

The wall stood without contest for 26 years. But, in the late 1980s, many Germans began openly criticizing the wall's presence. In 1987, US President Ronald Reagan delivered a speech in front of the wall, in honor of Berlin's 750th anniversary. In this speech, President Reagan made a bold appeal to the Premier of the Soviet Union, Mikhail Gorbachev, when he said, "Mr. Gorbachev, tear down this wall!"

Finally, two years later, in 1989, the people of East Berlin could bear it no longer. They began protesting the wall's existence in September of that year. On November 9th, 1989, crowds of people approached the wall with hammers, chisels, and other tools, and began destroying the wall by hand.

The Berlin Wall had endured for 28 years, but it was finally torn down. To this day, the towering and divisive structure remains one of the most chilling and powerful memories of those who lived through the Cold War.

Multiple Choice: Please answer the following questions related to the passages you just read:

1._____ What did Richard Nixon do in July of 1959?
a. He accused President Eisenhower of being a communist
b. He visited the Soviet Union and met with the Soviet Premier
c. He crashed the U-2 during a flight over the Soviet Union
d. He visited China, meeting with communist leader Mao Tse Tung

2._____ Who was the Premier of the Soviet Union during Nixon's visit in 1959?
a. Joseph Stalin   c. Leonid Brezhnev
b. Mikhail Gorbachev   d. Nikita Khrushchev

3._____ What was the significance of the Kitchen Debate?
a. The American people gained respect for Richard Nixon because they saw him standing up for American values
b. It became clear that that the Soviets had far superior home labor-saving technologies
c. An agreement was reached between the two sides which limited the number of nuclear weapons each would possess
d. The two leaders became furious with each other and immediately declared war between the two nations

4._____ What was the importance of Nikita Khrushchev's visit to the United States in 1959?
a. It was during his visit that Khrushchev declared war on the United States
b. It was the last time a Soviet Premier would ever visit the United States
c. It was the first time a Soviet Premier had ever visited the United States
d. It was a secret meeting, in which the leaders of the two nations negotiated peace

5._____ Which of the following correctly identifies how Khrushchev felt after his visit to the US?
a. He felt that war between the two nations was inevitable
b. He believed that the Soviet Union was superior and the US was not a threat
c. He felt that the two nations had a good chance of achieving peaceful cooperation
d. He believed that the Soviet Union could never begin to challenge the US

6._____ Lockheed developed this aircraft for the US in the 1950s.
a. F-102   c. U-2
b. F-106   d. B-52

7._____ What was the purpose of the plane mentioned in the previous question?
a. It was a bomber, designed to deliver a first strike against the Soviet Union
b. It was a spy plane, intended to spy on the Soviet Union
c. It was a super speed plane, built with the intent of breaking world speed records
d. It was a fighter, built to combat Soviet fighters in dogfights

8._____ Why did the U-2 flights prove important?
a. The US was able to prove that the Soviet military was not as powerful as everyone thought it was.
b. The Soviet Union never provoked an attack, because they feared the awesome power of this airplane.
c. These flights proved that the sound barrier could be broken.
d. The US realized that the Soviets had far superior weaponry and they would never be able to compete.

9._____ What happened to Gary Powers?
a. He was the first pilot to break the sound barrier.
b. The U-2 he was flying was shot down over the Soviet Union, and he was captured.
c. He became the first American to leave the Earth's atmosphere.
d. His efforts led to the first real peace treaty between the US and the Soviet Union.

10._____ What was the significance of the incident mentioned in the previous question?
a. Breaking the sound barrier made the idea of international flights practical.
b. Leaving the Earth's atmosphere led to an eventual colonization of the moon.
c. The first treaty between the US and the Soviet Union eventually led to world peace.
d. After the U-2 was shot down, relations between the US and the Soviet Union were shattered.

11._____ Which nations assisted West Germany?
a. The US & the United Kingdom   c. Italy & Switzerland
b. The Soviet Union & the US   d. Canada & Japan

12._____ Why were people defecting from East Germany and not returning?
a. Because a deadly plague had inflicted the East Germans
b. Because the East German government had encouraged many people to leave
c. Because the conditions in East Germany continued to worsen
d. Because the West Germans had promised a free home to all those who defected

13._____ The most well-known crossing point between East Berlin and West Berlin was?
a. The Iron Curtain   c. Checkpoint Brandenburg
b. The Berlin Crossing   d. Checkpoint Charlie

14._____ Which US President said, "Mr. Gorbachev, tear down this wall!"?
a. Ronald Reagan   c. Richard Nixon
b. Jimmy Carter   d. Dwight Eisenhower

15._____ In November of 1989, what happened to the Berlin Wall?
a. It was fortified with a new steel wall and machine gun emplacements.
b. It was bombed by a joint strike force of US and UK airplanes.
c. It was torn down by the people of Germany, using hammers and chisels.
d. It was accidentally destroyed during a drill by the Soviet Army.

Free Response Questions for The Kitchen Debate, the U-2, and the Berlin Wall:

1) Do you believe that a leader of a country visiting a rival nation is a good way to ease tense relations? If the citizens of the two nations fear conflict with one another, do you think friendly and publicized meetings between their leaders do much to ease public distrust? Why or why not?

2) Do you think that one nation actively spying on another is a violation of trust or not? Or is it a necessary evil if the two nations are adversaries? Explain your answer.

3) Can you imagine what it would be like to have family and friends living in the same city as you but not being allowed to see them? What, if anything, would you attempt to do about it if protesting the policy might endanger your life, or the lives of your loved ones? Explain your response.

Cold War Vocabulary: The Kitchen Debate, the U-2, and the Berlin Wall

a. The U-2
b. Ronald Reagan
c. Kitchen Debate
d. Cooperation
e. Defection

f. Gary Powers
g. Premier
h. Checkpoint Charlie
i. Nikita Khrushchev
j. The Berlin Wall

1._____ Leader of the Soviet Union from 1953 to 1964.

2._____ Constructed to separate East and West Berlin.

3._____ The U-2 pilot who was shot down over the Soviet Union and captured.

4._____ A desertion of allegiance or duty.

5._____ The title given to the leader of the Soviet Union.

6._____ A famous meeting where Richard Nixon and Nikita Khrushchev debated the positive and negative aspects of their nations.

7._____ Working together for a common purpose.

8._____ The most well-known crossing point along the Berlin Wall.

9._____ A plane designed by the United States in an effort to spy on the Soviet Union.

10._____ The US President who challenged Soviet leaders to tear down the Berlin Wall.

52 | P a g e   R e a d i n g   T h r o u g h   H i s t o r y

Cold War Vocabulary: Fill in the Blank

Use the words from the word bank, and write in the correct choice to complete the sentence.

a. The U-2
b. Ronald Reagan
c. Kitchen Debate
d. Cooperation
e. Defection

f. Gary Powers
g. Premier
h. Checkpoint Charlie
i. Nikita Khrushchev
j. The Berlin Wall

1. East Germans constructed _____, an 87-mile-long barrier between East and West Berlin.

2. In 1959, the Soviet _____ visited the United States for the first time.

3. The Berlin Wall was built to help end the _____ of those escaping East Germany.

4. Most Americans and other foreigners entering East Berlin did so at _____.

5. President Eisenhower and Vice President Richard Nixon both had meetings with Soviet Premier _____.

6. _____ was capable of flying fourteen miles high.

7. U-2 pilot _____ was captured by the Soviet Union.

8. Vice President Richard Nixon became popular in the United States after standing up to Premier Khrushchev during the _____.

9. US President _____ delivered a speech in front of the Berlin Wall and made the challenge that it be torn down.

10. After meeting with President Eisenhower, Premier Khrushchev believed he could achieve peaceful _____ with the United States.

Nikita Khrushchev

Following Joseph Stalin's death in 1953, the rest of the world was introduced to the new leader of the Soviet Union, Nikita Khrushchev. It was Khrushchev who guided the Soviet Union through many of the events of the 1950s and '60s.

Nikita Khrushchev was born in 1894, in a Russian village near the Ukrainian border. In 1918, he joined the Bolsheviks who were attempting to take control of the country. The Russian Civil War resulted in the Bolsheviks seizing power and creating the Soviet Union.

His involvement with the Bolsheviks, now known as the Communist Party, led to a flourishing political career in which he rose quickly through the party ranks. As early as 1932, he was attending private meetings with Joseph Stalin, eventually becoming one of the Premier's most trusted advisers.

In 1939, Khrushchev was sent to Ukraine where he oversaw part of The Great Purge in which millions of innocent Ukrainians were killed for being "enemies of the state". During World War II he was present during the defense of the city of Stalingrad, the most significant battle of the war in Russia.

After the war, as Stalin's health began to fail, Khrushchev advised the aging Premier. In 1953, after Stalin's death, Khrushchev emerged as the new leader and would serve as Premier of the USSR for the next ten years.

From the start, Khrushchev acted to separate himself from the years of tyranny carried out by his predecessor. He brought an end to the political trials and executions that had become common under Stalin. He granted a modest amount of freedom in the arts and literature and allowed Soviet citizens to travel to foreign countries. Tourists were also allowed to visit the Soviet Union as well.

One of Khrushchev's greatest successes was the Soviet space program. The Soviet Union became the first nation to launch a manmade satellite into orbit, as well as being the first with a man in space.

While Premier, Khrushchev had many dealings with the United States. Vice President Richard Nixon visited the Soviet Union in 1959 and met with Premier Khrushchev. In turn, Khrushchev visited the US within that same year.

Khrushchev is most noted for the role he played during the Cuban Missile Crisis. He and the American President John F. Kennedy worked out a deal to narrowly avoid a nuclear showdown between the two nations. As a result of the Cuban Missile Crisis, Khrushchev negotiated, and signed, a partial ban against testing nuclear weapons. The ban forbade all nuclear testing unless it took place below ground.

In 1964, members of his own Communist Party moved against him and forced him to resign the position of Soviet Premier. He retired to a quiet, private life and lived out his remaining years until he died from heart disease in 1971.

President John F. Kennedy

John Fitzgerald Kennedy was the 35th President of the United States. He is usually regarded as one of our most popular and well-remembered chief executives. How did President Kennedy achieve such a distinguished status?

John Kennedy was born in Massachusetts in 1917, the son of Joseph Kennedy and Rose Fitzgerald. He was the second of what would eventually be four brothers (his brothers were Joseph Jr., Robert and Teddy).

He enrolled at Harvard in 1936 and earned a spot on the varsity swim team, eventually graduating with a degree in International Affairs. In 1941, when the United States entered World War II, John joined the Navy and served with distinction throughout the war. He received the Navy and Marine Corp medal, as well as a Purple Heart and three bronze stars.

Following World War II, Kennedy ran for the House of Representatives and won. He served as a Representative for the State of Massachusetts for six years before being elected to the U.S. Senate in 1952. While working in the Senate, he wrote his book, Profiles in Courage, which won a Pulitzer Prize.

In 1960, he made the decision to run for President. His opponent was the popular Vice President Richard Nixon. The two candidates fought a hard-contested campaign. It proved to be one of the closest elections in the history of the nation, but in the end, John Kennedy had won by a very narrow margin, becoming the 35th President of the United States of America.

While President, Kennedy had several accomplishments as well as setbacks. His major accomplishments included beginning America's efforts to land a man on the moon and establishing the Peace Corps. The most significant setback was his administration's aiding of a group of Cuban refugees with a failed invasion of Cuba in 1961, known as the Bay of Pigs.

However, Kennedy's presidency is probably best remembered for the events that occurred in October of 1962. During the Cuban Missile Crisis it was discovered that the Soviet Union was establishing nuclear missile bases in Cuba. President Kennedy's management of the situation, and the avoidance of nuclear war, earned the young president adoration from countless Americans.

Unfortunately, on November 22nd, 1963, during a visit to Dallas, TX, a former marine named Lee Harvey Oswald shot President Kennedy from the window of a building known as the Texas School Book Depository. Kennedy died from his wounds and was succeeded by the Vice President, Lyndon B. Johnson.

The nation and much of the free world mourned the loss of President Kennedy. He had only been President of the United States for three years but had endeared himself to the hearts of the American people.

Multiple Choice: *Please answer the following questions related to the passages you just read:*

1._____ In the early stages of his political career, Nikita Khrushchev served as an advisor to?
a. Vladimir Lenin   c. Ivan the Terrible
b. Joseph Stalin   d. Richard Nixon

2._____ As a military advisor, Nikita Khrushchev was present during this important WWII battle.
a. Battle of the Bulge   c. Stalingrad
b. Leningrad   d. Normandy

3._____ What year did Nikita Khrushchev become the Premier of the Soviet Union?
a. 1951   c. 1959
b. 1953   d. 1961

4._____ As Premier of the Soviet Union, Khrushchev differed from Joseph Stalin in what way?
a. He was far more brutal than Stalin, holding fake trials and executing anyone he deemed
as being a threat.
b. He invited American leaders to the USSR and was able to end the nuclear standoff with them.
c. He closed the Soviet Union up tight, not allowing anyone to enter or leave.
d. He distanced himself from the policies of Stalin and brought an end to the political trials
and executions.

5._____ How did Nikita Khrushchev's career as Soviet Premier end?
a. He died of heart disease in 1971
b. Members of his own Communist Party forced him to resign
c. He was assassinated by Lee Harvey Oswald
d. The Soviet Union collapsed in 1991

6._____ During World War II, what branch of the military did John Kennedy serve in?
a. Army   c. Air Force
b. Navy   d. Marines

7._____ What was the title of John Kennedy's Pulitzer Prize-winning book?
a. Profiles in Courage   c. The Audacity of Hope
b. Heart of Darkness   d. A Time to Heal

8._____ Who was John Kennedy's opponent in the 1960 Presidential election?
a. Dwight D. Eisenhower   c. Harry S. Truman
b. Lyndon B. Johnson   d. Richard M. Nixon

9._____ The failed invasion of Cuba in 1961 was known as?
a. The Cuban Missile Crisis   c. The Bay of Pigs Invasion
b. The Caribbean Invasion   d. The Castro Insurgence

10._____ What won President Kennedy the adoration of countless Americans in 1962?
a. The success of the Bay of Pigs Invasion
b. President Kennedy's handling of the Cuban Missile Crisis
c. American astronauts landing on the moon
d. President Kennedy's establishment of the Peace Corps

Free Response Questions for Nikita Khrushchev & John F. Kennedy

1. Despite the fact that John F. Kennedy was president for only three years, he remains one of the most revered chief executives in US history. Using the content from the lesson as your guide, explain why you believe he remains one of the most popular US Presidents of all time.

2. How did Nikita Khrushchev and Joseph Stalin differ in their management of the Soviet Union? How, if any at all, do you believe the events of the Cuban Missile Crisis might have differed had Stalin been in charge of the USSR rather than Khrushchev?

3. Compare and contrast the lives of John F. Kennedy and Nikita Khrushchev. List three ways they were similar. List three ways in which they were different.

Cold War Vocabulary: Nikita Khrushchev & John F. Kennedy

a. Chief Executive   f. Accomplishment
b. Premier   g. Peace Corps
c. Resign   h. Adoration
d. Succeed   i. Candidate
e. Tyranny   j. Predecessor

1._____ The title given to the leader of the Soviet Union.

2._____ A person who seeks an office or position.

3._____ To formally give up an office or position.

4._____ An important achievement.

5._____ An unrestrained use of power.

6._____ The person who held an office before another.

7._____ A civilian organization sponsored by the US government, in which volunteers are sent to underdeveloped countries, and help the people of those nations.

8._____ The act of showing devoted honor or loyalty.

9._____ To follow or replace someone at a certain position or office.

10._____ A term used to describe the President of the United States, while fulfilling his duties as the head of the Executive Branch.

Cold War Vocabulary: Fill in the Blank
Use the words from the word bank, and write in the correct choice to complete the sentence.

a. Chief Executive   f. Accomplishment
b. Premier   g. Peace Corps
c. Resign   h. Adoration
d. Succeed   i. Candidate
e. Tyranny   j. Predecessor

1. Nikita Khrushchev attempted to distance himself from the _____ of Joseph Stalin.

2. John F. Kennedy's success handling the Cuban Missile Crisis earned him much _____ from many young Americans.

3. Nikita Khrushchev was the _____ of the Soviet Union following the death of Joseph Stalin.

4. Richard Nixon was the _____ who opposed John F. Kennedy in the Presidential election of 1960.

5. John F. Kennedy was a popular and well-remembered _____.

6. One of Kennedy's major accomplishments was starting an organization known as the _____.

7. Lyndon B. Johnson would _____ John F. Kennedy as President, after Kennedy was shot in Dallas, Texas.

8. Khrushchev proved to be a very different type of leader than his _____.

9. Under Khrushchev's leadership, the Soviet Union became the first nation to launch a manmade satellite. This was seen as a major _____.

10. In 1964, Premier Khrushchev was forced to _____.

Fidel Castro

Fidel Castro was one of the most enduring figures of the Cold War. But, who was Fidel Castro, and how did he acquire the position he held?

Fidel Castro was born in Cuba, in August of 1926. He attended the University of Havana, where he became interested in political matters. After college, he became involved with revolutions and rebellions in the Dominican Republic and Colombia.

In the early 1950s, he became convinced that the Cuban president, Fulgencio Batista, needed to be overthrown. Castro led a failed attack in 1953, which led to a one year imprisonment. After his release, he traveled to Mexico with his brother Raul and fellow revolutionary Ché Guevara.

In Mexico, Castro assembled a fighting force of 80 men and purchased an old yacht. Armed with 90 rifles, 40 pistols, and three machine guns, he began the 1,200 mile journey back to Cuba.

Upon returning to Cuba, Castro and Guevara took key roles in the war against Batista, finally overthrowing him in 1959. After Batista's ouster, Fidel Castro seized control of the government, becoming the Prime Minister (and eventually President).

The US Government distrusted Castro and attempted to remove him from power. This incident was known as the Bay of Pigs Invasion. Cuban exiles supported by the US invaded Cuba, hoping that the Cuban people would rise up and overthrow Castro. When this did not happen, the exiles were defeated easily.

Following the Bay of Pigs Invasion, Castro declared that Cuba would become a communist nation, and he allied himself with the Soviet Union. He allowed the Soviets to place nuclear missile bases in Cuba, causing the events that were eventually known as the Cuban Missile Crisis.

Castro continued to consolidate his power in Cuba, becoming a dictator. Those who spoke out against Castro's policies were arrested. Some estimates claim that as many as 15,000 Cubans were executed because of their opposition to Castro. Those not executed were placed in unsanitary prisons where they were beaten, tortured, and interrogated.

Others who opposed Castro attempted to escape. Utilizing small boats or rafts, they braved a difficult journey through the Caribbean Sea in an effort to reach the United States. It's estimated that approximately 1.2 million Cubans have left the island for the US since Castro gained power.

In 2008, due to his age and poor health, Fidel Castro relinquished his control over Cuba, handing the reigns of the government over to his brother Raul Castro.

The Bay of Pigs

In April of 1961, an incident known as the Bay of Pigs Invasion occurred. But what was the Bay of Pigs Invasion, and why did it happen?

Fidel Castro had taken control of the Cuban government in 1959, and the United States did not approve of Castro's leadership. In March of 1960, President Dwight Eisenhower approved a plan which had the objective of removing Castro from power, and $13 million was set aside for this purpose.

Initially, they had simply planned on supplying guerilla fighters with food and ammunition, but by late October, it was apparent that these efforts would not succeed. Therefore, the Central Intelligence Agency (CIA) developed a new plan to launch an amphibious assault against Cuba with 1,500 men.

President Eisenhower approved this plan and intended to recommend it to his successor, John Kennedy, who was preparing to take office. In January of 1961, President Kennedy was briefed on the situation and authorized the departments to continue.

The CIA began recruiting Cuban exiles (those who had fled Cuba and Castro) to make up the invading army. They were trained for several months and nicknamed themselves Brigade 2506. They rallied around former Cuban Prime Minister José Miró Cardona, who was slated to replace Castro if the invasion succeeded.

As the time for the invasion drew closer, the Cuban Government learned of the operation due to spies living in the US, as well as the Cuban exiles who bragged of their training and the planned invasion. Because the plan was so well known, the Cuban military was able to prepare.

The initial attack began on April 15th, 1961. Eight B-26s, painted to appear as if they were part of the Cuban Air Force, bombed three different airfields. Air attacks continued for two more days. During that time, American UN Ambassador Adlai Stevenson and President Kennedy both maintained that the United States was not involved, insisting that the attacks were strictly being conducted by Cuban exiles.

The actual invasion started on the 18th of April, and the fighting lasted three days. From the outset, the exiles were outnumbered, and they were eventually overwhelmed. After running out of ammunition, 1,202 members of Brigade 2506 were captured and held as prisoners. They were placed on trial and convicted of treason before being sentenced to 30 years in prison. After lengthy negotiations, 1,113 of the prisoners were returned to the US in exchange for $53 million worth of food and medicine.

The Bay of Pigs Invasion was a severe failure. Five Americans and 114 Cuban exiles died. One hundred and seventy six members of the Cuban Armed Forces died as well, not to mention hundreds of other Cubans. The incident proved a major embarrassment for President Kennedy and made him and his advisers very wary of becoming involved in Cuban affairs again.

Multiple Choice: *Please answer the following questions related to the passages you just read:*

1._____ In what three nations was Fidel Castro involved in revolutions with?
a. Cuba, the Dominican Republic & Colombia
b. Cuba, Haiti & the Dominican Republic
c. Cuba, Chile & Venezuela
d. Cuba, Haiti & the Dominican Republic

2._____ In what country did Fidel Castro arm and prepare for his takeover of Cuba?
a. Venezuela   c. Argentina
b. Chile   d. Mexico

3._____ What was the United States' response to Castro's seizing of power in Cuba?
a. They supported him, even sending Cuban exiles to aid him.
b. They distrusted him and supported a group of Cuban exiles who tried to overthrow him.
c. They felt neutral about him, and tried to ignore what was going on in Cuba.
d. They did not know what to think about him, but immediately sent dignitaries to establish relations with his new government.

4._____ What type of political freedoms/civil liberties did the Castro regime establish in Cuba?
a. He allowed many political liberties and freedoms, and people were permitted to openly speak out against the government.
c. He allowed for freedom of speech, as long as you did not criticize his government directly.

b. Those who spoke out against Castro's policies were arrested and as many as 15,000 Cubans were said to have been executed.
d. He allowed limited political and civil freedoms, gradually expanding and giving more freedoms to his people over time.

5._____ What type of government did Fidel Castro establish in Cuba?
a. Socialist   c. Democratic
b. Communist   d. Constitutional Monarchy

6._____ Which US President initially authorized the planning for the Bay of Pigs Invasion?
a. John F. Kennedy   c. Lyndon B. Johnson
b. Dwight D. Eisenhower   d. Richard M. Nixon

7._____ The Bay of Pigs Invasion was planned and overseen by which US government agency?
a. CIA   c. IRS
b. FBI   d. FEMA

8._____ The Bay of Pigs Invasion was carried out by which group?
a. Mexican Freedom Fighters   c. Haitian Rebels
b. The Green Berets   d. Cuban Exiles

9._____ The most accurate date for the Bay of Pigs Invasion is?
a. July 20, 1969   c. April 18, 1961
b. November 22, 1963   d. February 3, 1959

10._____What happened to the Cuban exiles that were captured following the Bay of Pigs Invasion?
a. They were placed on trial, and imprisoned, but eventually returned to the US.
b. They were all executed.
c. They were placed on trial, and held in prison for 30 years.
d. They were given the choice to join the Cuban Army. If they refused, they were tortured.

Free Response Questions for Fidel Castro & The Bay of Pigs Invasion:

1. In 1953, Fidel Castro failed in an attempted coup to overthrow the government in Cuba. Describe the punishment he received for this failed effort. Do you feel this punishment was too severe, too lenient, or proper? Explain your answer.

2. Do you believe the US Government had a responsibility to attempt and oust Fidel Castro from power in Cuba, since he had established such a friendly relationship with the Soviet Union and his island nation sat a mere 90 miles from the United States? Why or why not?

3. It is believed that more than 1.2 million Cubans have fled Cuba for the United States since Castro came to power. If you were in their situation, would you attempt fleeing (you can be executed for it), or would you attempt to change the political situation in Cuba from within? State your reasoning and how you would go about doing it.

Vocabulary: Fidel Castro & The Bay of Pigs Invasion

a. assemble
b. exiles
c. utilize
d. consolidate
e. guerrilla

f. amphibious
g. interrogate
h. treason
i. incident
j. relinquish

1._____ A betrayal of one's own nation.

2._____ Those who have been banished from their native country.

3._____ The use of unconventional tactics in warfare.

4._____ Occurring or functioning on both land and water.

5._____ To put to use.

6._____ To examine by asking questions.

7._____ An occurrence or event.

8._____ To bring together; unite.

9._____ To let go of or release

10._____ To gather in one place.

Cold War Vocabulary: Fill in the Blank
Use the words from the word bank, and write in the correct choice to complete the sentence.

a. assemble
b. exiles
c. utilize
d. consolidate
e. guerrilla

f. amphibious
g. interrogate
h. treason
i. incident
j. relinquish

1. The Bay of Pigs Invasion was to be an _____ assault.

2. Fidel Castro went to Mexico, where he could _____ a fighting force of 80 men.

3. The United States was supplying _____ fighters who were attempting to overthrow Castro.

4. After Fidel Castro took control of Cuba, he continued to _____ his power.

5. Those who attempted to overthrow Castro were Cuban _____ living in Florida.

6. Castro would imprison and _____ anyone who disagreed with his policies.

7. The soldiers who were captured after the Bay of Pigs Invasion were placed on trial and convicted of _____.

8. Many Cubans who disagreed with Castro, would _____ small boats and try to escape Cuba.

9. The Bay of Pigs Invasion was an embarrassing _____ for the Kennedy administration.

10. Because of his failing health, Fidel Castro had to _____ his control over the Cuban government in 2008.

The Cuban Missile Crisis

In 1959, Fidel Castro took control of the island nation of Cuba, some 90 miles from the State of Florida. He established Cuba as a communist nation and began forging a close relationship with the Soviet Union, which concerned the United States.

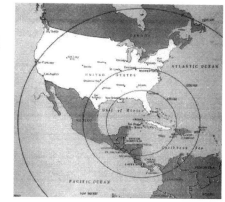

In April of 1961, the US made an attempt to remove Castro from power. The US trained Cuban exiles who had escaped Castro by moving to Florida and supported them in an invasion of Cuba. This became known as "The Bay of Pigs Invasion". The invasion failed, and Castro continued to tighten his grip over Cuba.

In August of 1962, the Cubans and Soviets began secretly establishing sites to launch nuclear missiles from Cuba. With the use of these missile bases, the Soviet Union could have first strike capability against the United States.

On October 15th, the United States discovered the existence of these missiles. President John F. Kennedy and his advisers considered several different strategies ranging from diplomacy (talking to the Soviets), to a blockade, or even a full scale invasion of Cuba.

President Kennedy eventually chose a blockade. The US Navy placed ships in the Caribbean Sea, surrounding Cuba, and would not allow any Soviet ships to reach Cuba. On October 22nd, Kennedy announced the threat to the nation, causing panic and turmoil across the country.

Throughout the next several days, the crisis continued to escalate as both sides refused to back down. The United States insisted that the missile bases be removed, while the Soviet Union and Cuba refused to admit that the bases even existed.

As the days continued, the Soviet Union remained diligent, and the Kennedy administration began preparing the early stages of an invasion plan. On October 25th, the blockade was challenged for the first time. Soviet ships approached the quarantine zone, but American ships held their ground. The Soviet vessels were forced to turn back, and the blockade continued.

On that same day, the US Ambassador to the United Nations, Adlai Stevenson, confronted the Soviets in the UN assembly, revealing photographic evidence that forced the Soviet Union to admit the missile bases existed.

The crisis finally ended on October 28, 1962 when President Kennedy and Soviet Premier Nikita Khrushchev reached a secret agreement. The Soviets would remove their missile bases in Cuba. In exchange, the US would remove missile bases in Turkey (which were close to the Soviet Union's borders).

John F. Kennedy

To this day, the Cuban Missile Crisis is regarded as the closest that the US has ever come to a nuclear war. The event was one of the most intense moments in the relationship between the United States and the Soviet Union and one of the defining moments of the Cold War.

Cuban Missile Crisis: Public Reaction

When President John F. Kennedy announced that US intelligence had revealed that the Soviet Union was setting up nuclear missile sites in Cuba, there were many different types of reactions from the American public.

Kennedy informed the American people on the evening of October 22, 1962, and the initial reaction most experienced was a sudden state of shock. They listened in fascination and horror as the President announced his intentions to set up a quarantine around the tiny island nation of Cuba.

However, as the days progressed, and the Crisis worsened, public reaction turned from shock to panic. Many citizens truly believed that a nuclear exchange was imminent, and therefore, did everything they could to prepare for such an eventuality.

Grocery and supply stores were overwhelmed with customers racing for items the public felt it needed. Families began stockpiling nonperishable food and supplies such as water, toilet paper, flashlights, and batteries.

Some families constructed fallout shelters and stockpiled supplies inside of them. Unfortunately, most couldn't afford shelters, so they stockpiled their necessities inside basements or another location in or near their home.

Many saw religious implications in the global events that were unfolding. They were certain that the approach of nuclear war signaled the beginning of "the end of the world". Special church services were held during the crisis, and many sought to confess their sins before any bombs began falling.

Aside from the panic, there was also a wave of protests that swept across the nation. Angry citizens protested against nuclear weapons, declaring that these dangerous devices would eventually lead to the death of everyone. Also, a small minority believed the US was acting as the aggressor in this situation and that America should simply leave Cuba alone.

These were just a few of the various reactions to the Cuban Missile Crisis. Each person, and family, reacted in their own unique way.

Name_____

Multiple Choice: *Please answer the following questions related to the passages you just read:*

1._____ Who took control of Cuba in 1959?
a. Nikita Khrushchev   c. Fidel Castro
b. Poncho Villa   d. Che Guevara

2._____ The failed attempt to overthrow Castro in 1961 is known as?
a. The Bay of Pigs Invasion   c. The Cuban-American War
b. The Cuban Missile Crisis   d. The Battle of the Caribbean

3._____ After learning of the Soviet missile bases in Cuba, what course of action did President Kennedy decide to take?
a. He called for an all-out invasion to remove Castro from power.
b. He authorized use of the atomic bomb to destroy Cuba.
c. He immediately began disarmament talks with the Soviet Union.
d. He called for a quarantine, or blockade around Cuba.

4._____ How was the Cuban Missile Crisis resolved?
a. The Soviets agreed to remove their missile bases, and, in exchange, the US agreed to remove missile bases in Turkey.
b. An all-out war erupted between the US and the Soviet Union, with thousands of casualties on both sides.
c. A universal disarmament treaty was signed, and since that day neither nation has possessed nuclear weapons.
d. The situation was never resolved, and the two nations have been engaged in a tense standoff for over fifty years.

5._____ What is one of the reasons why the Cuban Missile Crisis is significant?
a. It was the last time that either nation threatened the other with nuclear weapons.
b. It was a major breakthrough in the eventual peace between the two nations.
c. It is usually considered the closest that the US and the Soviet Union ever came to nuclear war.
d. It represented the beginning of the Cold War.

6._____ Who was President of the United States during the
                  Cuban Missile Crisis?
a. Dwight Eisenhower   c. Lyndon Johnson
b. John Kennedy   d. Richard Nixon

7._____ What types of supplies did people stockpile during the
                  Cuban Missile Crisis?
a. Food, water, toilet paper, flashlights and batteries
b. Luxury items such as designer clothing and fine silks
c. Cuban cigars and other items that could only be found in Cuba
d. Guns, ammunition, and armor

8._____ If families could not afford a fallout shelter, where might they
                  store their supplies?
a. In the trunk of their car   c. Under their beds
b. Buried in their backyard   d. In their basement

9._____ Why were many people going to churches during the
                  Cuban Missile Crisis?
a. Because churches were giving away free supplies to help survive the crisis.
b. Many believed that churches would be the only safe place in the event of a
    nuclear strike.
c. Churches had been designated as rescue centers for those who no longer
    had a home after an attack.
d. Many believed the end of the world was near, and they wanted to confess
    their sins.

10._____ What was one reason that some were protesting during the
                  Cuban Missile Crisis?
a. They believed that the US should immediately surrender to the
    Soviet Union.
b. They believed that nuclear weapons would eventually be the end of us all.
c. They believed that the nuclear weapons were causing global warming.
d. They believed that President Kennedy should be removed from office
    because of his poor handling of the situation.

Free Response Questions for the Cuban Missile Crisis and Public Reaction

1) Assume you were the head of state of a powerful nation and discovered that a rival country was placing offensive weapons and bases in a potentially hostile nation bordering your country. How would you respond? Explain your answer.

2) The Cuban Missile Crisis was resolved through a secret negotiation between President Kennedy and Premier Khrushchev. In exchange for the Soviets removing the missiles from Cuba, the US agreed to remove their Jupiter missiles from Turkey within six months. Do you feel that such an agreement (working without the public or the US Congress) was the proper strategy? Why or why not?

3) Public reactions to the fear caused by the Cuban Missile Crisis varied greatly from community to community and family to family. How would you respond (what would you do) if a potentially catastrophic and seemingly unavoidable event had people fearing, talking, and acting like the end of civilization was at hand?

Cold War Vocabulary: The Cuban Missile Crisis and Public Reaction

a. Imminent
b. Exiles
c. Diplomacy
d. Fidel Castro
e. Stockpiled

f. Bay of Pigs
g. Quarantine
h. Commotion
i. Escalate
j. Aggressor

1._____ The leader of Cuba who established a communist government.

2._____ To increase in intensity and magnitude.

3._____ A person, group or nation that attacks first or initiates hostilities.

4._____ Great disturbance or upheaval; disorder.

5._____ A strict isolation imposed on a region or person.

6._____ Government officials conducting peaceful relations with officials of another nation.

7._____ An unsuccessful invasion of Cuba, which had the purpose of removing Fidel Castro from power.

8._____ Accumulated a large supply for future use.

9._____ Likely to occur at any moment.

10._____ People who have been banished from their native land.

Name_____

Cold War Vocabulary: Fill in the Blank
Use the words from the word bank, and write in the correct choice to complete the sentence.

a. Imminent
b. Exiles
c. Diplomacy
d. Fidel Castro
e. Stockpiled

f. Bay of Pigs
g. Quarantine
h. Commotion
i. Escalate
j. Aggressor

1. The President and his advisers considered many options, including
_____, a blockade or even an invasion of Cuba.

2. President Kennedy chose to place a blockade, or _____
around the island of Cuba.

3. Some people felt that the US was acting as the _____
during the Cuban Missile Crisis.

4. Many people _____ supplies in their basements,
fearing a nuclear war would happen soon.

5. The _____ invasion did not succeed in removing
Castro from power.

6. When President Kennedy announced that the Soviet Union was establishing nuclear
missile bases in Cuba, it caused much panic and _____.

7. Many citizens believed that a nuclear exchange was _____.

8. For several days after President Kennedy made the announcement regarding the
Soviet missiles in Cuba, the situation continued to _____.

9. In 1959, _____ took control of Cuba.

10. The Bay of Pigs invasion was carried out by Cuban _____
who were hoping to reclaim their nation from Fidel Castro.

The Vietnam Conflict

The Vietnam Conflict was one of the longest, bloodiest struggles of the Cold War era. So, how did it start? How long did it last?

What most people call the Vietnam War began in 1946, and at the time, was known as the Indochina War. French forces fought against rebelling forces known as the Viet Minh. The two sides fought for nearly ten years, and the end result was the creation of two nations, North Vietnam and South Vietnam.

North Vietnam was led by its founder Ho Chi Minh who desired to gain control of the entire former French colony and institute communism nationwide. South Vietnam, under Ngo Dinh Diem, had established a republic. In 1959, North Vietnam, aided by the Soviet Union, attacked South Vietnam.

Ho Chi Minh

The United States saw this as a Soviet effort to expand communism and, throughout the early 1960s, sent soldiers to South Vietnam, in the form of advisors, to assist in the training of South Vietnamese forces. By 1963, 16,000 Americans were stationed in Southeast Asia.

In August of 1964, two American ships were reportedly fired upon in the Gulf of Tonkin. This resulted in the US Congress passing the Gulf of Tonkin Resolution, which gave President Lyndon B. Johnson authority to conduct military operations in Vietnam (in order to protect US personnel). The first American combat troops arrived in 1965.

Throughout South Vietnam, North Vietnamese supporters, known as the Viet Cong, fought a guerrilla war against US and South Vietnamese troops. A guerrilla war is one in which "hit and run" tactics are used in order to avoid a direct military confrontation. The North Vietnamese Army also engaged in a more traditional, drawn out war against American forces.

US involvement in Vietnam reached its peak with a Viet Cong attack known as the Tet Offensive (it occurred during the Vietnamese holiday known as Tet). The Vietnam Conflict was widely covered by the American media, and the effectiveness of the well-organized Tet Offensive by enemy forces greatly damaged public support for US involvement in the conflict.

Following this incident, the US began the process of Vietnamization. This meant gradually turning the war over to the South Vietnamese as US soldiers were slowly withdrawn. The fighting officially stopped in January of 1973 with the signing of the Paris Peace Accords. Once US forces were completely withdrawn, the North Vietnamese resumed their attacks, and Vietnam was reunited as a communist nation, which it still remains today.

Throughout the Vietnam Conflict, well over a million Vietnamese died. 58,000 American soldiers also lost their lives.

Name_____

Multiple Choice: Please answer the following questions related to the passage you just read:

1._____ Who was the leader of North Vietnam?
a. Chiang Kai Shek   c. Cho En Lai
b. Mao Tse Tung   d. Ho Chi Minh

2._____ What was the significance of the Gulf of Tonkin Resolution?
a. It brought the Vietnam Conflict to its conclusion
b. It gave President Johnson the authority to conduct military operations in Vietnam
c. It officially divided Vietnam into two separate nations, North and South Vietnam
d. It authorized the use of nuclear weapons, which led to millions of deaths

3._____ Who were the Vietcong?
a. They were North Vietnamese supporters fighting in South Vietnam
b. They were Koreans who were fighting in support of South Vietnam
c. They were a group of top-notch Vietnamese scientists working on a secret weapon
d. They were the leaders of the South Vietnamese government

4._____ What is a guerrilla war?
a. A war in which large apes are trained to do the fighting instead of people
b. A war in which there is no actual fighting, only espionage and threats
c. A war in which hit and run tactics are used frequently
d. A war in which the two nations have used nuclear weapons repeatedly

5._____ What does the term "Vietnamization" mean?
a. This was a term used to identify who enemy soldiers were.
b. This was a term used to describe American soldiers who decided not to return home after the conflict had ended.
c. This was a term used to describe the communist takeover of North Vietnam.
d. This was a term used to describe the process of gradually turning the war over to the South Vietnamese.

Free Response Questions for the Vietnam Conflict:

1) In your opinion, with the Soviet Union backing the communist North Vietnamese, should the United States have been willing to commit combat troops to the jungles of Southeast Asia in order to prevent communism from expanding and taking hold there? Explain your answer.

2) After reading about guerilla warfare tactics, why do you think a smaller or ill-equipped force might choose to implement them? Do you believe it is a good strategy? What types of environments (desert, jungle, mountains, etc.) do you feel it would be the most effective in? Why?

3) Public support for US efforts in Vietnam dwindled after the Tet Offensive, despite the fact that American troops held their ground and inflicted major casualties on the Viet Cong. Most credit this loss of support to nightly news coverage showing rather graphic images and giving daily counts of US troop casualties. In your opinion, why would such thorough news coverage impact the public's support of the war in a negative way?

Cold War Vocabulary: The Vietnam Conflict

a. Ho Chi Minh
b. Indochina War
c. Paris Peace Accords
d. Gulf of Tonkin
e. Tet Offensive

f. Gulf of Tonkin Resolution
g. Vietnamization
h. Guerrilla War
i. Viet Minh
j. Viet Cong

1._____ The name given to those who opposed the French during the Indochina War.

2._____ An attack by the North Vietnamese which occurred during the Vietnamese New Year holiday.

3._____ A location where two American ships were allegedly fired upon, which led to further US involvement in the Vietnam Conflict.

4._____ The leader of North Vietnam, who established communism in that nation.

5._____ The war fought between the French and the Vietnamese from 1946 to 1954.

6._____ This gave President Johnson the authority to conduct military operations in Vietnam.

7._____ Term given to the policy of slowly turning the war over to the South Vietnamese and withdrawing American troops.

8._____ Supporters of North Vietnam, fighting in South Vietnam.

9._____ The treaty which officially brought the fighting to an end in Vietnam.

10._____ A war in which "hit and run" tactics are used.

Cold War Vocabulary: Fill in the Blank
Use the words from the word bank, and write in the correct choice to complete the sentence.

a. Ho Chi Minh
b. Indochina War
c. Paris Peace Accords
d. Gulf of Tonkin
e. Tet Offensive

f. Gulf of Tonkin Resolution
g. Vietnamization
h. Guerrilla War
i. Viet Minh
j. Viet Cong

1. Throughout the Vietnam Conflict, the Viet Cong fought a _____ against the US and the South Vietnamese forces.

2. In the late 1940s and early 1950s, the French were fighting against the _____.

3. In August of 1964, two American ships were reported as being attacked in the _____.

4. The French and the Viet Minh fought against each other in the _____.

5. The guerilla war in South Vietnam was fought by the _____.

6. The first American combat troops arrived in Vietnam in 1965 following the passage of the _____.

7. Following the Tet Offensive, the US began the slow process of _____.

8. US involvement in the Vietnam Conflict reached its peak after an attack by the North Vietnamese known as the _____.

9. The communist leader of North Vietnam was _____.

10. American troops did not actually leave Vietnam until after the signing of the _____.

The Space Race

One of the most symbolic representations of the Cold War was the competition between the USSR and the USA as they raced each other into space. How did this "space race" get started? How did it end?

On October 4th, 1957, the Soviets became the first nation to launch an artificial satellite into orbit around the planet. This satellite, a large metal sphere about the size of a beach ball, was known as Sputnik 1. With the successful launch of Sputnik, the "space race" had begun.

America quickly responded. Within four months, the first US satellite, Explorer 1, achieved orbit around the Earth.

However, the US had always thought of itself as the leader in rocket development and space technology. Therefore, the fact that the Soviets had achieved this feat first greatly disturbed many Americans. In fact, many citizens panicked, viewing this as proof that the American education system was far behind that of the Soviets. School curriculum was carefully examined, placing a stronger emphasis on science and mathematics courses.

The following year, the National Aeronautics and Space Administration (NASA) was created to help the United States more effectively achieve its goals in space.

In April of 1961, Soviet cosmonaut Yuri Gagarin became the first man to orbit the planet. Once again, the United States had been beaten into space. One month later, Alan Shepard became the first American in space, but, the US did not have a man orbit the planet until nearly a year later, when John Glenn accomplished the feat.

On May 25, 1961, President John F. Kennedy made a bold announcement that the United States would make it a goal to land a man on the moon before the end of the decade. Needless to say, since the US had stated this as their goal, the USSR also began making plans to put a man on the moon.

Throughout the decade of the 1960s, both the Americans and the Soviets experienced many successes and failures in their efforts to reach the moon. The most tragic event occurred in 1967. In January of that year, three American astronauts were killed in a fire while onboard the Apollo 1 spacecraft. In April of 1967, the Soviets also lost their first cosmonaut who died while attempting re-entry into the Earth's atmosphere.

Finally, in 1969, the Apollo 11 mission saw the US win the race to the moon. The craft was commanded by Neil Armstrong, along with crewmates Edwin "Buzz" Aldrin and Michael Collins. On July 20th, 1969, Neil Armstrong became the first human to set foot on the surface of the moon. As he did so, he spoke his famous line, "That's one small step for man; one giant leap for mankind."

With the astronauts' arrival on the moon, the space race effectively came to an end. Both the Soviet Union and the United States would continue their space programs, but many of the early goals had already been achieved.

Multiple Choice: Please answer the following questions related to the passages you just read:

1._____ The first Soviet satellite was known as?
a. Eagle I
c. Sputnik I
b. Explorer I
d. Cosmonaut I

2._____ What was the American reaction to the launch of the
Soviet satellite?
a. Most Americans did not care, they were too busy with their lives to notice.
b. Many Americans panicked, fearing that America's school curriculum was not difficult enough.
c. The US military immediately shot down the Soviet satellite.
d. Americans reacted with contempt; they knew the Soviets could not compete with the US in the space race.

3._____ The first human to orbit the planet was?
a. Yuri Gagarin
c. Chuck Yeager
b. Neil Armstrong
d. Alan Shepard

4._____ What is the significance of John Glenn?
a. He was the first man to walk on the moon
b. He was the US President who started America's space program
c. He was the primary designer of all of America's space technology
d. He was the first American to orbit the Earth

5._____ Why is Neil Armstrong significant?
a. He was the first man to walk on the moon
b. He was a top-ranking general who ordered a halt to the space program
c. He was the director of NASA
d. He was the first American astronaut

Free Response Questions for the Space Race:

1) After the Soviets managed to get an early lead in the Space Race, the United States restructured their education system and placed a greater emphasis on math and science courses in the public schools. Which school subjects do you think should be stressed the most and why?

2) After reading the Space Race and other lessons thus far, do you feel that the rivalry between the US and the USSR helped to advance the two nations and push them forward in any way? If so, what are some examples of this? If not, explain why you feel it is not the case.

3) Do you feel that the United States should strive to be the world leader in satellite technology and space exploration? If so, should agencies such as NASA receive more funding, or should the undertaking be turned over to privately-owned companies? Explain your answers.

Cold War Vocabulary: The Space Race

a. Explorer I
b. Alan Shepard
c. Apollo 11
d. Neil Armstrong
e. Sputnik

f. Yuri Gagarin
g. NASA
h. John Glenn
i. Curriculum
j. Satellite

1._____ The first artificial satellite launched into orbit by the Soviet Union.

2._____ The first American to orbit the planet.

3._____ A natural or artificial object that revolves around a larger object in space.

4._____ The administration created to help the United States achieve its goals in space.

5._____ The first American satellite launched into orbit.

6._____ The first man to walk on the moon.

7._____ The first American in space.

8._____ The regular course of study in schools.

9._____ The spacecraft which carried the first astronauts to land on the moon.

10._____ A Soviet cosmonaut who became the first man to orbit the planet.

Cold War Vocabulary: Fill in the Blank
Use the words from the word bank, and write in the correct choice to complete the sentence.

a. Explorer I
b. Alan Shepard
c. Apollo 11
d. Neil Armstrong
e. Sputnik

f. Yuri Gagarin
g. NASA
h. John Glenn
i. Curriculum
j. Satellite

1. The space race began when the Soviet Union launched _____.

2. Sputnik was the first artificial (or manmade) _____
to orbit the Earth.

3. The Americans responded to Sputnik by launching their own satellite known as
_____.

4. Americans panicked after the launch of Sputnik and restructured school
_____ to place more emphasis on science and math courses.

5. The United States created a government agency known as _____
to help them accomplish their goals in space.

6. The Soviet cosmonaut _____ became the first man in
space as well as the first to orbit the planet.

7. The first American in space was _____.

8. _____ became the first American to orbit the planet.

9. Neil Armstrong, Buzz Aldrin, and Michael Collins traveled to the moon in
_____.

10. As _____ stepped onto the moon, he said, "That's one small
step for man, one giant leap for mankind."

Nixon Goes to China

Why would a staunch, anti-communist American President visit the world's most populous communist nation? That's precisely what happened in early 1972.

President Richard Nixon had long been known for his strong anti-communist stance. He had assisted Senator Joseph McCarthy during the Red Scare era and had been selected as the Vice President in 1952, largely because of his firm anti-communist position. Many Americans also remembered him for standing up to Soviet Premier Khrushchev in 1959, during the famous Kitchen Debate.

Mao Tse Tung with Richard Nixon

So, for many, it seemed unusual when President Nixon decided to make a journey to Communist China. In February of 1972, Nixon traveled to Beijing and became the first American President to visit mainland China while in office.

Nixon met with the aging Chairman Mao Tse Tung who had made China a communist nation in 1949. Nixon also traveled to several different locations, including the Great Wall, Hangzhou, and Shanghai. While President Nixon met with Chinese leaders, the First Lady (Pat Nixon) toured schools, factories, and hospitals.

At the conclusion of the week, the US and China agreed to open trade and other relations between the two nations. President Nixon referred to his week in China as "the week that changed the world" and stated that he hoped it would help end 22 years of hostility between the two nations. The US would eventually establish full diplomatic relations with China in 1979.

The meeting had a profound impact on the Cold War. With Nixon's successful visit to China, he managed to make the world's most populated nation a potential ally. It effectively placed China and the United States on the same side by souring Soviet relations with the Chinese.

China remains a communist nation to this day, but, thanks to Nixon's policies, the United States and China are strong economic partners. Since the 1990s, China has held the most favored nation trading status with the United States. In 2011, the US bought more than 1.3 trillion dollars' worth of goods from Communist China.

Chairman Mao

In popular culture, this visit has given rise to the expression, "Only Nixon can go to China". This phrase is typically used when someone (usually a politician) is acting in an uncharacteristic fashion.

Strategic Arms Limitation Talks

In the 1970s, the United States and the Soviet Union began to realize the dangers of nuclear weapons and the threats that accompanied them. In an effort to make the world safer and ease tensions, the two nations attempted to take steps to limit the numbers of these weapons. So, what steps did they take? Did these steps work?

The first negotiations between the two nations to limit nuclear arms occurred in Helsinki, Finland, in 1969. These discussions began in November of that year, but failed because both governments harbored strong opinions regarding how many nuclear weapons each country should be allowed to have.

Over the course of the next three years, the two sides had a series of meetings in Helsinki, Finland and Vienna, Austria. These discussions came to be known as the Strategic Arms Limitation Talks (more commonly known as SALT).

Carter and Brezhnev signing SALT II

After years of failed negotiations, the first real progress came in 1971when the two nations reached an agreement to limit the number of anti-ballistic missile systems each of them had, somewhat easing the tension between the two super powers.

In 1972, President Richard Nixon and Soviet Premier Leonid Brezhnev gave one another assurances that they would halt the number of ballistic missile launchers at existing levels and dismantle many of the older bases designed for launching longer-range inter-continental ballistic missiles (or ICBMs).

Several years later, a second round of negotiations occurred. These discussions became known as the Strategic Arms Limitation Talks II (SALT II). These discussions took place from 1977 to 1979 between US President Jimmy Carter and Soviet Premier Brezhnev.

The results of SALT II were a series of promises by both sides to limit the production of new nuclear weapons. Each nation agreed to produce and maintain no more than 2,250 of each type of nuclear missile.

Despite their best efforts, the SALT negotiations were not entirely successful because neither nation honored the agreement. Six months after SALT II was signed, Soviet troops invaded Afghanistan, straining the delicate relationship between the US and the USSR. Soviet military personnel were also discovered operating on the island of Cuba, and the final SALT treaty was never ratified by the US Senate due to the heightened irritation with the USSR.

In 1986 President Ronald Reagan formally withdrew the United States from SALT II after accusing the Soviet Union of violating the pact.

The Collapse of the Soviet Union

The Soviet Union existed from 1922 to 1991. So, how did the Soviet Union come to an end? Why did it collapse?

The beginning of the end of the Soviet Union came in 1985 when a man named Mikhail Gorbachev became premier. When Gorbachev came to power, he implemented several new governmental policies. These changes collectively became known as perestroika, which means "restructuring". Many believe perestroika helped bring about the end of the USSR.

Mikhail Gorbachev

One of the most important things he did was ease the restrictions on free speech. For many, many years, the Soviet people had not been allowed to speak out against the government for fear of severe punishment. Under perestroika, they were able to speak their mind more openly.

Through a policy known as glasnost, the government became more open as well. Glasnost is a Russian term which means "openness". It referred to an increased amount of transparency of government activities (they would no longer hide information from the people).

The economic situation in the Soviet Union was also very grim during this time. Many people were poor, and they began using their newfound freedom of speech to speak out against the miserable condition communism had left them in. These were feelings many had wanted to express for decades, but had not been allowed to do so.

The civil unrest that led to the downfall of the Soviet Union began in the outer-regions of the country. Estonia was the first region where organized protest movements began demanding independence from the Soviet Union. Before long, similar protest erupted in Lithuania, Latvia, Azerbaijan, Georgia, Ukraine, Moldova, and Belarus. Unlike similar incidents from the past, Premier Gorbachev did not attempt to end the protests with the Soviet Army.

In 1991, as it seemed that the Soviet Union was on the verge of falling apart, a group of hard line, devout Communists attempted a "coup d'état" (coo- day-tah), meaning they attempted to seize control of the government. When the people learned this had happened, they took to the streets by the thousands. Massive protests erupted in Moscow and other major cities.

In an effort to maintain power, the Communists sent out the military. However, troops refused to raise their weapons against the people, and many joined the protests. The Communists realized that without the military, their coup would fail. Power was returned to Gorbachev.

Within months after the failed coup, the Soviet Union collapsed entirely. In December of 1991, Premier Gorbachev stepped down, and in January of 1992, the Soviet Union ceased to exist.

The collapse of the Soviet Union was seen as a triumph of freedom and democracy over totalitarianism. With the death of the Soviet Union, the era known as the Cold War finally came to an end.

Multiple Choice: Please answer the following questions related to the passages you just read:

1._____ In February of 1972, Richard Nixon became the first American President to do what?
a. Travel across the ocean on an airplane
b. Travel to China while in office
c. Leave Earth's atmosphere in a space shuttle
d. Address the nation on television

2._____ Who did President Nixon meet with shortly after arriving in China?
a. Chairman Mao Tse Tung   c. General Douglas MacArthur
b. Ho Chi Minh   d. Emperor Hirohito

3._____ What was the result of Richard Nixon's visit to China?
a. The United States and China declared war on one another
b. An assassination attempt was made on Nixon by a violent faction of Chinese rebels
c. The United States and China opened trade relations with each other
d. Richard Nixon realized that the United States could never compete with China

4._____ What impact did this meeting have on the Cold War?
a. It brought the Cold War to a conclusion after the US and China signed a peace treaty
b. It placed China and the United States on the same side, opposing the Soviet Union
c. It caused the US and China to declare war on each other after negotiations failed
d. The meetings had little or no impact on the Cold War

5._____ Why was President Nixon acting out of character by visiting China?
a. Nixon rarely left the United States and feared flying
b. Nixon had openly stated many times that he did not like Chinese food
c. Nixon was well known for opposing communists on many previous occasions
d. Nixon was a recluse and rarely left the White House

6._____ What do the initials MAD stand for?
a. Militarized Armed Defense   c. Mutually Assured Destruction
b. Monetary Assistance Department   d. Metro Automobile Department

7._____ What was the significance of the "talks" which started in Helsinki, Finland in 1969?
a. The purpose of the talks was to limit strategic arms
b. The purpose of the talks was a peace treaty between the US and the Soviet Union
c. The purpose of the talks was to bring an end to the Vietnam Conflict
d. The purpose of the talks was to negotiate the release of hostages the Soviets had taken

8._____ What do the initials SALT stand for?
a. Standard Armored Light Tank
b. Soviet-American Labor Talks
c. Space and Aeronautics Limitations Treaty
d. Strategic Arms Limitation Talks

9._____ Which two leaders signed the SALT II treaty?
a. Jimmy Carter & Leonid Brezhnev
b. Richard Nixon & Mao Tse Tung
c. Richard Nixon & Nikita Khrushchev
d. Dwight Eisenhower & Nikita Khrushchev

10._____ Why were the SALT negotiations not entirely successful?
a. Neither nation honored their half of the agreement
b. The treaty was too demanding and neither side could live up to it
c. Other nations put pressure on them to abandon the treaty
d. A major war between the US, Soviet Union and China ruined the negotiations

11._____ What is the significance of Mikhail Gorbachev?
a. He became the Soviet Premier in 1985, and many of the changes he made led to the collapse of the Soviet Union
b. He was a general who overthrew the Soviet Premier in the late 1980s
c. He was the Soviet Ambassador to the United States who helped the Americans avoid war throughout the Cold War
d. He was a Soviet pilot who was shot down over the United States. His capture led to a full-scale war between the US and the Soviet Union

12._____ What does Glasnost mean?
a. It was a Russian term which meant "war"
b. It was a German term which meant "bread"
c. It was a Russian term which meant "peace"
d. It was a Russian term which meant "openness"

13._____ In 1991, a group of hardline communists attempted a coup d'état. What does this mean?
a. They tried to perform a ritual 40 day fasting, which ended in starvation
b. They attempted to take control of the government
c. They attempted to flee the country and defect to the United States
d. They tried to surrender their nation to the United States

14._____ Why were many of the protests throughout the Soviet Union successful?
a. The military refused to raise their weapons and some even joined the protesters
b. The protests were peaceful in nature, and were not seen as a threat by the military
c. Soviet officials had been bribed so that the protests could continue as planned
d. The protests were not successful. They were brutally put down by the military

15._____ What year did the Soviet Union finally collapse?
a. 1985   c. 2001
b. 1979   d. 1991

Free Response Questions for Nixon goes to China, SALT, and The Collapse of the Soviet Union

1) The United States and Communist China have managed to remain strong economic partners, particularly since the 1990s, despite their different political and economic systems. Why do you feel that the United States could not achieve such a relationship with the Communist Soviet Union?

2) Despite years of negotiations, the Soviet Union and the United States both failed to live up to their obligations and restrictions placed upon them in the SALT agreements. Why do you believe each nation felt that they had to do so? How important do you think it is to honor an agreement, even if you suspect that the other party is failing to do so?

3) Mikhail Gorbachev's policies of glasnost and perestroika are largely credited with leading to the downfall of the Soviet Union. How important do you feel that liberties such as freedom of speech, press, religion, and assembly are to the happiness of a people? Which freedom do you believe is the most important and why?

Cold War Vocabulary: Nixon goes to China, SALT, and the collapse of the Soviet Union

a. Chairman Mao
b. Coup d'état
c. Mikhail Gorbachev
d. SALT
e. Richard Nixon

f. MAD
g. Leonid Brezhnev
h. Perestroika
i. Detente
j. Glasnost

1._____ The American President who visited China in 1972.

2._____ The leader of the People's Republic of China. He established China as a communist nation in 1949.

3._____ A nuclear arms limitation treaty signed by the US and the Soviet Union in 1972.

4._____ The leader of the Soviet Union in the 1970s. He signed both SALT treaties.

5._____ Soviet leader in the 1980s who made changes which helped bring about the end of the Soviet Union.

6._____ Seizing control of the government from those in power.

7._____ A policy which insured that each nation had enough nuclear weapons to destroy the other side.

8._____ A Russian term which means openness.

9._____ A Russian term meaning restructuring.

10._____ A French term meaning relaxation.

Cold War Vocabulary: Fill in the Blank
Use the words from the word bank, and write in the correct choice to complete the sentence.

a.   Chairman Mao
b.   Coup d'état
c.   Mikhail Gorbachev
d.   SALT
e.   Richard Nixon

f.   MAD
g.   Leonid Brezhnev
h.   Perestroika
i.   Detente
j.   Glasnost

1. Throughout much of the Cold War, the US and the Soviet Union practiced a policy of _____, or Mutually Assured Destruction.

2. In the late 1960s and early 1970s, the Soviet Union and the United States began a series of discussions known as _____.

3. President _____ made a historic trip to China and opened trade relations with that nation.

4. _____ was the aging leader of China who met with Nixon in 1972.

5. The relationship between the US and the Soviet Union through the 1970s was best characterized with the word _____, which means relaxation.

6. A group of devout communists attempted a _____ to remove Mikhail Gorbachev from power.

7. In the 1970s, _____, the Premier of the Soviet Union, signed two arms limitation treaties with the United States.

8. Many believe that the restructuring of the Soviet government in the mid-1980s, known as _____, had much to do with the eventual downfall of the Soviet Union.

9. _____ was the Premier of the Soviet Union during its collapse.

10. In the 1980s, the Soviet Union promised to hide less information from its people and other nations. This policy became known as _____, which means openness.

Name_____

The Cold War: Final Test

Multiple Choice: *Please answer the following questions:*

1._____ The title of the book written by Karl Marx and Friedrich Engels was?
   a.   Crime and Punishment
   b.   The Wealth of Nations
   c.   The Communist Manifesto
   d.   Birth of a Nation

2._____ Which of the following is true in a communist nation?
   a.   Personal freedom and liberty are highly valued
   b.   All property and businesses are owned by the national government
   c.   Distribution of products is not regulated by the government
   d.   Employees have a wide range of salaries depending on the job they perform

3._____ The first nation in which a communist revolution took place was?
   a.   Russia
   b.   Germany
   c.   France
   d.   The United States of America

4._____ The modern day nations of Russia, Ukraine, Belarus and twelve others created what nation?
   a.   The Warsaw Pact
   b.   The Soviet Union
   c.   The Holy Roman Empire
   d.   The Eurasian Alliance

5._____ The initials USSR stand for?
   a.   Union of the Socialist States of Russia
   b.   United States of Socialist Russia
   c.   Union of the Soviet Socialist Republics
   d.   Unified States of Socialist Regions

6._____ In 1924, who became the leader of the Soviet Union?
   a.   Vladimir Lenin
   b.   Leon Trotsky
   c.   Nikita Khrushchev
   d.   Joseph Stalin

7._____ Which of the following events occurred in 1991?
   a.   1991 was the year the Soviet Union was created.
   b.   1991 was the year the US and the Soviet Union officially opened trade relations.
   c.   1991 was the year the Soviet Union collapsed.
   d.   1991 was the year when war began between the US and the Soviet Union.

8._____ What was the American and British response to the Soviet blockade of West Berlin?
   a.   The Berlin Airlift
   b.   A declaration of war
   c.   The surrendering of West Berlin to the Soviet Union
   d.   Military buildup along the border between the two halves of Germany

9._____ Winston Churchill was the first to use this phrase to describe the relationship between Western and Eastern Europe.
   a.   The Great Divide
   b.   The Iron Curtain
   c.   The Iron Cross
   d.   The Stone Wall

10._____ The initials NATO stand for?
  a. North American Treaty Organization
  b. National American Transit Operation
  c. National Aeronautic Tactical Outpost
  d. North Atlantic Treaty Organization

11._____ The Warsaw Pact nations were located where?
  a. Eastern Europe   c. South America
  b. Western Europe   d. Africa

12._____ America's policy towards communism throughout most of the Cold War
            was known as?
  a. The Marshall Plan   c. The Monroe Doctrine
  b. The Truman Doctrine   d. The Roosevelt Corollary

13._____ The policy of 'containment' was an effort to contain what?
  a. They were attempting to contain a dangerous disease which had affected several
      countries in Southeast Asia.
  b. They were attempting to contain a radiation leak which threatened to
      contaminate several rivers.
  c. They were attempting to contain communism and prevent it from spreading to
      other nations.
  d. They were attempt to contain a flood, which was threatening to engulf several
      major cities.

14._____ If one nation fell to communism, other nations in the same region would
            also fall. This theory was known as?
  a. The Slippery Slope Theory   c. The Avalanche Theory
  b. The Chain Reaction Theory   d. The Domino Theory

15._____ What was the Marshall Plan?
  a. An assistance program to help the nations of Western Europe rebuild.
  b. An invasion plan created for a possible attack on the Soviet Union.
  c. A plan designed to help poor American families purchase new homes.
  d. A plan which would help citizens respond in the event of a nuclear attack.

16._____ Which two major military conflicts resulted because of the
            containment policy?
  a. World War I & World War II   c. Korean Conflict & Vietnam Conflict
  b. World War II & Korean Conflict   d. Vietnam Conflict & Gulf War

17._____ Which nation supported North Korea in its effort to become a
            communist nation?
  a. Japan   c. The Soviet Union
  b. Germany   d. Vietnam

18._____ This location was the border between North and South Korea.
  a. Korea Bay   c. 38th Parallel
  b. 48th Parallel d. Sea of Japan

19._____ The leader of North Korea was?
   a. Ngo Dinh Diem
   b. Mao Tse Tung
   c. Ho Chi Minh
   d. Kim Il Sung

20._____ Why did President Harry Truman remove Douglas MacArthur from command in Korea?
   a. General MacArthur had attempted to seize command from President Truman.
   b. General MacArthur was deemed to be mentally unfit for duty.
   c. General MacArthur was killed in action and therefore had to be replaced.
   d. General MacArthur had provoked the Chinese into entering the war.

21._____ The heavily fortified border between North and South Korea is known as?
   a. The Berlin Wall
   b. The Demilitarized Zone
   c. The Sudetenland
   d. The Great Divide

22._____ Who was Mao Tse Tung?
   a. He was the leader of the Chinese Communists during the Chinese Civil War.
   b. He was a religious leader who encouraged the Chinese to avoid war at all cost.
   c. He was the leader of the Chinese Nationalists during the Chinese Civil War.
   d. He was an influential writer who encouraged the Chinese to attack the United States.

23._____ Which of the following best describes The Long March?
   a. The Chinese forced prisoners to march across the Gobi Desert.
   b. A springtime offensive by the Chinese Nationalists, which lasted throughout the month of March.
   c. A retreat by the Chinese Communists, which lasted well over a year.
   d. The victorious march by the Chinese Communists as they approached Beijing.

24._____ The Chinese Nationalist Party eventually fled to this location.
   a. Taiwan
   b. Thailand
   c. Vietnam
   d. Japan

25._____ After taking control China, what did the communists officially rename it?
   a. The Republic of China
   b. The People's Republic of China
   c. The Communist Chinese Republic
   d. The Soviet Chinese Union

26._____ What is the significance of Senator Joseph McCarthy?
   a. In the early 1950s, he began accusing many people of being communists.
   b. He was accused of being a Soviet spy and sentenced to a life in prison.
   c. He replaced Douglas MacArthur as the new commander in Korea.
   d. He developed the hydrogen bomb, which became an important weapon during the Cold War.

27._____ What did the initials HUAC stand for?
   a. Housing & Urban Access Committee
   b. Hispanic Unified Artists Coalition
   c. House Unethical Activities Committee
   d. House Un-American Activities Committee

28._____ If the Loyalty Review Board found someone to be "Un-American", what might the consequence be?
   a.   The person's position would be terminated.
   b.   The person would be immediately deported.
   c.   The person would be placed in a re-education center.
   d.   The person would be forced to undergo a series of psychological examinations.

29._____ This couple became the only Americans to receive the death penalty for being spies.
   a.   Pierre & Marie Curie   c.   Julius & Ethel Rosenberg
   b.   John & Jane Doe   d.   Mike & Suzy Johnson

30._____ What was the name of the animated character that taught students about nuclear safety?
   a.   Bugs Bunny   c.   Smilin' Joe Fusion
   b.   Tommy the Atom   d.   Bert the Turtle

31._____ Where were children instructed to hide during an air raid drill?
   a.   In a closet   c.   In the restroom
   b.   Under their desks   d.   In the frame of a doorway

32._____ The radioactive ash created by a nuclear explosion is known as what?
   a.   Toxic Waste   c.   Nuclear Ash
   b.   Fallout   d.   Radiated Debris

33._____ What feature would help a building be designated as a fallout shelter?
   a.   High ceilings and a balcony
   b.   A walk-in safe and very few windows
   c.   Carpet flooring and large restrooms
   d.   Large basements with thick concrete walls

34._____ Why did some families build fallout shelters in the middle of the night?
   a.   The soil was easier to dig into during the night
   b.   It was less expensive to hire a night time work crew
   c.   They feared that the communists might be spying on them
   d.   They did not want their neighbors to know they had a shelter

35._____ What was the significance of the two radio stations 640 and 1240 AM?
   a.   Those stations were well-known for broadcasting baseball games.
   b.   Those stations were dedicated to broadcasting anti-communist propaganda.
   c.   Those stations were the civil defense stations, which would broadcast important information in the event of an attack.
   d.   Those stations were the only stations allowed to broadcast a Presidential address.

36._____ Who was the Premier of the Soviet Union during Nixon's visit in 1959?
   a.   Joseph Stalin   c.   Leonid Brezhnev
   b.   Mikhail Gorbachev   d.   Nikita Khrushchev

37._____ What was the purpose of the U-2 plane?
a.   It was a bomber, designed to deliver first strike capabilities against the Soviet Union.
b.   It was a plane built to spy on the Soviet Union.
c.   It was a super speed plane, built with the intent of breaking world speed records.
d.   It was a fighter, built to combat Soviet fighters in dogfights.

38._____ Why were people defecting from East Germany and not returning?
a.   Because a deadly plague had inflicted the East Germans.
b.   Because the East German government had encouraged many people to leave.
c.   Because the conditions in East Germany continued to worsen.
d.   Because the West Germans had promised a free home to all those who defected.

39._____ Which US President said, "Mr. Gorbachev, tear down this wall!"?
a.   Ronald Reagan   c.   Richard Nixon
b.   Jimmy Carter   d.   Dwight Eisenhower

40._____ In November of 1989, what happened to the Berlin Wall?
a.   It was fortified with new steel and machine gun emplacements.
b.   It was bombed by a joint strike force of US and UK airplanes.
c.   It was torn down by the people of Germany, using hammers and chisels.
d.   It was accidentally destroyed during a drill by the Soviet Army.

41._____ Who took control of Cuba in 1959?
a.   Nikita Khrushchev   c.   Fidel Castro
b.   Poncho Villa   d.   Che Guevara

42._____ The failed attempt to overthrow Fidel Castro in 1961 is known as?
a.   The Bay of Pigs Invasion   c.   The Cuban-American War
b.   The Cuban Missile Crisis   d.   The Battle of the Caribbean

43._____ How was the Cuban Missile Crisis resolved?
a.   The Soviets agreed to remove their missile base, and, in exchange, the US agreed to remove a missile base in Turkey as well.
b.   An all-out war erupted between the US and the Soviet Union, with thousands of casualties on both sides.
c.   A universal disarmament treaty was signed, and since that day neither nation has possessed nuclear weapons.
d.   The situation was never resolved, and the two nations have been engaged in a tense standoff for over fifty years.

44._____ Who was President of the United States during the Cuban Missile Crisis?
a.   Dwight Eisenhower   c.   Lyndon Johnson
b.   John Kennedy   d.   Richard Nixon

45._____ What was the significance of the Gulf of Tonkin Resolution?
a.   It brought the Vietnam Conflict to its conclusion.
b.   It gave President Johnson the authority to conduct military operation in Vietnam.
c.   It officially divided Vietnam into two separate nations, North and South Vietnam.
d.   It authorized the use of nuclear weapons, which led to millions of deaths.

46._____ Who were the Vietcong?
   a.   They were North Vietnamese supporters fighting in South Vietnam.
   b.   They were Koreans who were fighting in support of South Vietnam.
   c.   They were a group of top-notch Vietnamese scientists working on a secret weapon.
   d.   They were the leaders of the South Vietnamese government.

47._____ The first Soviet satellite was known as?
   a.   Eagle I   c.   Sputnik I
   b.   Explorer I   d.   Cosmonaut I

48._____ In February of 1972, Richard Nixon became the first American
                  president to...
   a.   Travel across the ocean on an airplane.
   b.   Travel to China while in office.
   c.   Leave Earth's atmosphere in a space shuttle.
   d.   Address the nation on television.

49._____ What is the significance of Mikhail Gorbachev?
   a.   He became the Soviet Premier in 1985, and many of the changes he made led to
        the collapse of the Soviet Union.
   b.   He was a general who overthrew the Soviet Premier in the late 1980s.
   c.   He was the Soviet Ambassador to the United States who helped the Americans
        avoid a direct military confrontation with the Soviets.
   d.   He was a Soviet pilot who was shot down over the United States. His capture led
        to a full scale war between the US and the Soviet Union.

50._____ What year did the Soviet Union finally collapse?
   a.   1985   c.   2001
   b.   1979   d.   1991

Answer Key:

Communism & The Soviet Union:
Multiple Choice:

1) C
2) A
3) D
4) B
5) A
6) B
7) C
8) D
9) A
10) C

Free Response:

1. Student responses should demonstrate an understanding of the issues at hand. They should be able to defend/justify their answers.
2. Student responses should demonstrate an understanding of the issues. They should be able to defend their answers.
3. Students should be able to select a position on the questions and justify their choices.

Vocabulary:

1) E - Vladimir Lenin
2) C – Communism
3) G – Karl Marx
4) B – The Proletariat
5) J – Adversaries
6) H – Industrialization
7) I – The Communist Manifesto
8) F – Bolsheviks
9) D – The Soviet Union
10) A – Cold War

Vocabulary (Part Two):

1) The Proletariat
2) Cold War
3) Karl Marx
4) Vladimir Lenin
5) Adversaries
6) Communism
7) Bolsheviks
8) Industrialization
9) The Communist Manifesto
10) The Soviet Union

The Berlin Airlift & The Iron Curtain:
Multiple Choice:

1) B
2) C
3) A
4) D
5) A
6) B
7) C
8) D
9) A
10) C

Free Response:

1) Part 1 - Students should be able to describe the Berlin Airlift and the parties involved.
   Part 2 - Answers will vary, but students should be able to justify their choice.
2) Part 1 - Answers will vary but should demonstrate student understanding of the content.
   Part 2 - Responses will vary, but should show that students comprehend the material.
3) Part 1 - The Soviets hoped to counter the move made by the Allied Nations with their creation of NATO.
   Part 2 – Students should justify their responses.

Vocabulary:

1) E – Berlin Airlift
2) B – Isolated
3) G – Hostile
4) I – Necessities
5) A – Blockade
6) J – Casualties
7) F – Iron Curtain
8) C – Dictatorship
9) H – NATO
10) D – Warsaw Pact

Vocabulary (Part Two)

1) Necessities
2) Dictatorship
3) Hostile
4) NATO
5) Blockade
6) Berlin Airlift
7) Isolated
8) Casualties
9) Warsaw Pact
10) Iron Curtain

The Truman Doctrine:
Multiple Choice:

1) B
2) C
3) D
4) A
5) C

Free Response:

1) Part 1 - Truman concluded that the US should do everything within its power to assist these nations.
   Part 2 - Student responses should demonstrate an understanding of the issue.
2) Part 1 - The US gave the aid in hopes that it would help these nations resist communism and influence from the Soviet Union.
   Part 2 - Student responses should demonstrate an understanding of the issue.
3) Part 1 - Korea and Vietnam
   Part 2 - Student responses should demonstrate an understanding of the issue.

Vocabulary:

1) B – Harry Truman
2) H – Truman Doctrine
3) E – Containment
4) I – Domino Theory
5) G – The Marshall Plan
6) J – Implemented
7) C – Monetary
8) F – Prominent
9) A – Dominant
10) D – Turmoil

Vocabulary (Part Two):

1) Dominant
2) Truman Doctrine
3) The Marshall Plan
4) Domino Theory
5) Harry Truman
6) Implemented
7) Monetary
8) Turmoil
9) Containment
10) Prominent

The Chinese Civil War & The Korean Conflict:
Multiple Choice:

1) A
2) C
3) D
4) A
5) B
6) C
7) C
8) D
9) D
10) B

Free Response:

1) Part 1 - China was invaded by the Army of Japan and the two sides joined forces to defend China.
   Part 2 - Student responses should demonstrate an understanding of the communist/democratic issue or a leadership struggle.
2) Part 1 - MacArthur had criticized Truman for his handling of the war and also believed that the decision to use nuclear weapons should rest with him and not the President.
   Part 2 - Student responses should demonstrate an understanding of the issue.
3) Alike - Possible responses – Both were struggles in Asia between communist and democratic forces. China was involved. Students may provide other valid answers.
   Different - Possible responses – The Communist were fully victorious in China. The conflicts occurred in different countries. The US and other nations did not get involved in China. Students may provide other valid answers.

Vocabulary:

1) D – Chiang Kai Shek
2) F – Mao Tse Tung
3) E – The Long March
4) I – The People's Republic of China
5) J – The Republic of China
6) A – 38th Parallel
7) B – Kim Il Sung
8) H – Douglas MacArthur
9) C – Stalemate
10) G – The DMZ

Vocabulary (Part Two):

1) Kim Il Sung
2) Stalemate
3) Douglas MacArthur
4) The Long March
5) The People's Republic of China
6) The DMZ
7) Chiang Kai Shek
8) The Republic of China
9) 38th Parallel
10) Mao Tse Tung

Cold War Spies & The Red Scare:
Multiple Choice:

1) B
2) C
3) A
4) C
5) D
6) A
7) D
8) B
9) A
10) D
11) C
12) B
13) D
14) D
15) A

Free Response:

1) Student responses should demonstrate an understanding of the issue and their reasoning should be explained.
2) Students responses should be backed up by clear reasoning and argument.
3) Students should be encouraged to be creative, possibly even drawing their own movie poster. They should also demonstrate an understanding of Cold War era issues.

Vocabulary:

1) E – Joseph McCarthy
2) H – HUAC
3) I – Infiltrate
4) G – Blacklist
5) B – McCarthyism
6) A – Propaganda
7) F – Reds
8) D – Hysteria
9) J – Paranoia
10) C – Espionage

Vocabulary (Part Two):

1) Espionage
2) Joseph McCarthy
3) Infiltrate
4) McCarthyism
5) Blacklist
6) Hysteria
7) HUAC
8) Propaganda
9) Paranoia
10) Reds

School & Home Civil Defense:
Multiple Choice:

1) A
2) B
3) D
4) C
5) B
6) C
7) A
8) C
9) D
10) C

Free Response:

1) Student responses should demonstrate an understanding of agencies such as the FDCA and their reasoning for deciding yes or no should be explained.
2) Students responses should be backed up by clear reasoning and argument. Answers should include such logic as; kids would pay more attention to it, it would make them feel more comfortable with the threat, it could save their life, etc.
3) Part 1 - Students should explain their answers. Part 2 – Responses should include such examples as; serious injures for the first aid kit and storms for the basement.

Vocabulary:

1) D – Civil Defense
2) J – Pantry
3) H – Coordinate
4) F – Procedures
5) E – Non-perishable
6) I – Brochure
7) A – Block Warden
8) C – Debris
9) B – Precautions
10) G – Duck and Cover

Vocabulary (Part Two):

1) Duck and Cover
2) Precautions
3) Coordinate
4) Civil Defense
5) Debris
6) Procedures
7) Pantry
8) Non-perishable
9) Block Warden
10) Brochures

Fallout Shelters & Nuclear Effects:
Multiple Choice:

1) B
2) D
3) A
4) C
5) B
6) C
7) D
8) A
9) B
10) C
11) D
12) C
13) A
14) D
15) D

Free Response:

1) Responses will vary, but students should be able to describe some location that satisfactorily answers the question.
2) Student responses will vary. They should take the time to explain their answers.
3) Students should be able to select a position on the questions and justify their choice.

Vocabulary:

1) G – Fallout
2) D – CONELRAD
3) J – Accommodate
4) E – Geiger Counter
5) F – Radiation
6) A – Fallout Shelter
7) B – Dismantled
8) I – Surplus
9) H – Foxhole
10) C – Designated

Vocabulary (Part Two):

1) CONELRAD
2) Fallout
3) Accommodate
4) Geiger Counter
5) Designated
6) Fallout Shelter
7) Foxhole
8) Surplus
9) Radiation
10) Dismantled

The Kitchen Debate, The U-2, and The Berlin Wall:
Multiple Choice:

1) B
2) D
3) A
4) C
5) C
6) C
7) B
8) A
9) B
10) D
11) A
12) C
13) D
14) A
15) C

Free Response:

1) Responses will vary, but students should take a clear position on both issues and explain their answers.
2) Student responses will vary. They should take a position and defend their answer.
3) Students should be able to select a position and justify their choices.

Vocabulary:

1) I – Nikita Khrushchev
2) J – The Berlin Wall
3) F – Gary Powers
4) E – Defection
5) G – Premier
6) C – Kitchen Debate
7) D – Cooperation
8) H – Checkpoint Charlie
9) A – The U-2
10) B – Ronald Reagan

Vocabulary (Part Two):

1) The Berlin Wall
2) Premier
3) Defection
4) Checkpoint Charlie
5) Nikita Khrushchev
6) The U-2
7) Gary Powers
8) Kitchen Debate
9) Ronald Reagan
10) Cooperation

Nikita Khrushchev & John Kennedy:
Multiple Choice:

1) B
2) C
3) B
4) D
5) B
6) B
7) A
8) D
9) C
10) B

Free Response:

1. Answers could include but are not limited to; his assassination, role in the space race, and his role in ending the Cuban Missile Crisis peacefully. Students should explain their reasons clearly.
2. Part 1: Khrushchev ended the torture, trials, and executions of those who disagreed with him. He also opened up the country to foreign tourism and allowed Soviets to visit other nations, along with extending other greater freedoms to his country's citizens. Part 2: Students should display some reasoning and understanding of the policies and tactics of Joseph Stalin in their answers. There is no correct answer.
3. Answers could include but are not limited to the following. Alike; both leaders of their country, both had military backgrounds, both were involved in the Cuban Missile Crisis, both played a major role in the space race. Differences; Kennedy was assassinated, Kennedy was elected while Khrushchev was appointed, Khrushchev was an advisor to Stalin whereas Kennedy served in the US Senate, and Khrushchev was forced out of office and got to experience a short retirement.

Vocabulary:

1) B – Premier
2) I – Candidate
3) C – Resign
4) F – Accomplishment
5) E – Tyranny
6) J – Predecessor
7) G – Peace Corps
8) H – Adoration
9) D – Succeed
10) A – Chief Executive

Vocabulary (Part Two):

1) Tyranny
2) Adoration
3) Premier
4) Candidate
5) Chief Executive
6) Peace Corps
7) Succeed
8) Predecessor
9) Accomplishment
10) Resign

Fidel Castro & The Bay of Pigs:
Multiple Choice:

1) A
2) D
3) B
4) B
5) B
6) B
7) A
8) D
9) C
10) A

Free Response:

1. Student responses will vary, but they should explain their reasoning for choosing as they did.
2. Answers will vary, but students should back up their answers with clear reasoning.
3. Answers will vary but students should explain their reasons for choosing as they did and give some specific examples of how they would go about doing it.

Vocabulary:

1) H – Treason
2) B – Exiles
3) E – Guerrillas
4) F – Amphibious
5) C – Utilize
6) G – Interrogate
7) I – incident
8) D – Consolidate
9) J – relinquish
10) A – assemble

Vocabulary (Part Two):

1) Amphibious
2) Assemble
3) Guerrilla
4) Consolidate
5) Exiles
6) Interrogate
7) Treason
8) Utilize
9) Incident
10) Relinquish

Cuban Missile Crisis & Public Reaction:
Multiple Choice:

1) C
2) A
3) D
4) A
5) C
6) B
7) A
8) D
9) D
10) B

Free Response:

1) Responses will vary, but students should take a clear position and explain their answer.
2) Student responses will vary. They should take a clear position and defend their answer.
3) Students should be allowed freedom to respond to this question.

Vocabulary:

1) D – Fidel Castro
2) I – Escalate
3) J – Aggressor
4) H – Commotion
5) G – Quarantine
6) C – Diplomacy
7) F – Bay of Pigs
8) E – Stockpiled
9) A – Imminent
10) B – Exiles

Vocabulary (Part Two):

1) Diplomacy
2) Quarantine
3) Aggressor
4) Stockpiled
5) Bay of Pigs
6) Commotion
7) Imminent
8) Escalate
9) Fidel Castro
10) Exiles

Vietnam Conflict:
Multiple Choice:

1) D
2) B
3) A
4) C
5) D

Free Response:

1) Responses will vary, but students should take a clear position and explain their answer.
2) Student responses will vary. They should take a clear position on the questions and back their responses with logic.
3) Possible answers could include making the war more real to the public, citizens growing weary of the conflict, citizens seeing US casualties on the TV screen, a growing questioning of why US troops were involved, or that fact that they were seeing real combat footage unedited by the Department of Defense for the first time. Other answers are acceptable if they are backed by clear reasoning.

Vocabulary:

1) I – Viet Minh
2) E – Tet Offensive
3) D – Gulf of Tonkin
4) A – Ho Chi Minh
5) B – Indochina War
6) F – Gulf of Tonkin Resolution
7) G – Vietnamization
8) J – Viet Cong
9) C – Paris Peace Accords
10) H – Guerrilla War

Vocabulary (Part Two):

1) Guerilla War
2) Viet Minh
3) Gulf of Tonkin
4) Indochina War
5) Viet Cong
6) Gulf of Tonkin Resolution
7) Vietnamization
8) Tet Offensive
9) Ho Chi Minh
10) Paris Peace Accords

The Space Race:
Multiple Choice:

1) C
2) B
3) A
4) D
5) A

Free Response:

1) Responses will vary, but students should take a clear position and explain their answer.
2) Student responses will vary. Examples could include technology, education, stimulation of their economies, family safety, national security, patriotism, etc. Other responses will also be acceptable.
3) Student responses will vary, but reasonable responses should be given and explained.

Vocabulary:

1) E – Sputnik
2) H – John Glenn
3) J – Satellite
4) G – NASA
5) A – Explorer I
6) D – Neil Armstrong
7) B – Alan Shepard
8) I – Curriculum
9) C – Apollo 11
10) F – Yuri Gagarin

Vocabulary (Part Two):

1) Sputnik
2) Satellite
3) Explorer I
4) Curriculum
5) NASA
6) Yuri Gagarin
7) Alan Shepard
8) John Glenn
9) Apollo 11
10) Neil Armstrong

Nixon Goes to China; SALT; & The Collapse of the Soviet Union
Multiple Choice:

1) B
2) A
3) C
4) B
5) C
6) C
7) A
8) D
9) A
10) A
11) A
12) D
13) B
14) A
15) D

Free Response:

1) Responses will vary, but students should use clear reasoning when explaining their answer.
2) Student responses will vary. Examples could include technology, education, stimulation of their economies, family safety, national security, patriotism, etc. Other responses will also be acceptable.
3) Responses will vary, but students should give clear answers and defend at least one of the choices on the second question with logical reasoning.

Vocabulary:

1) E – Richard Nixon
2) A – Chairman Mao
3) D – SALT
4) G – Leonid Brezhnev
5) C – Mikhail Gorbachev
6) B – Coup d'état
7) F – MAD
8) J – Glasnost
9) H – Perestroika
10) I – Détente

Vocabulary (Part Two):

1) MAD
2) SALT
3) Richard Nixon
4) Chairman Mao
5) Détente
6) Coup d'état
7) Leonid Brezhnev
8) Perestroika
9) Mikhail Gorbachev
10) Glasnost

Cold War Final Test:

1) C
2) B
3) A
4) B
5) C
6) D
7) C
8) A
9) B
10) D
11) A
12) B
13) C
14) D
15) A
16) C
17) C
18) C
19) D
20) D
21) B
22) A
23) C
24) A
25) B
26) A
27) D
28) A
29) C
30) D
31) B
32) B
33) D
34) D
35) C
36) D
37) B
38) C
39) A
40) C
41) C
42) A
43) A
44) B
45) B
46) A
47) C
48) B
49) A
50) D